THE REBOOT

50 Dates with Myself

Marie MacMillan

ISBN-13: 978-1-945-587-44-3
Library of Congress Control Number: 2019915973
Marie MacMillan
The Reboot
1. Memoir; 2. Dating; 3. Portland, Oregon; 4. Self-care

Book design: Dancing Moon Press
Cover design: Dancing Moon Press
Cover Art: Lindy Martin

Manufactured in the United States of America
Dancing Moon Press
dancingmoonpress.com
Bend, Oregon

DANCING
MOON
PRESS

Contents

New beginnings are often disguised as painful endings.
-Lao Tzu

I will spare you the gory details of my own personal sob story. This is not a Nicholas Sparks heartbreak novel or a Shakespearean tragedy filled with death and unrequited love. This is not a tale about the breaking, but of the putting back together.

However, to shed light on this journey's origins, I suppose I must provide an historical element to give it perspective.

Mine is not a magnificently unique story of bitter misfortune or woefully doomed romance. It's pretty universally standard: Boy meets Girl (me), Girl and Boy start dating after two years of flirtatious friendship, Girl and Boy date seriously for two more years, Boy takes Girl on important trip to meet all of his family. Girl then naturally wants to start planning commitment of the matrimonial kind.

Boy says no. Girl confused.

Boy says he's not sure and needs more time.

Girl says that's bullshit.

Boy and Girl cannot agree and see everything going downhill fast…romantic checkmate, if you can imagine.

Girl and ~~Boy~~ Dufus decide to call it quits before they despise each other and irreversibly wreck each other's mental health, emotional state, and ability to function like normal adults.

Was it mutual? —Yes. Fault (and ultimately agreement) was found on both sides.

Do I resent the assessment that I wasn't "forever" material? —Very. Much. So.

Do I regret the decision to split up? —No, but that doesn't dull the inevitable shitty aftermath of pulling shattered pieces of myself back together.

That's all I'll say about the actual break-up, because it doesn't matter. The relationship was over. The ugly details of how and why don't matter. That's not what this story is about. As two wise writers wrote succinctly, it's called a break-up because it's broken[1] and it was time to move on.

Okay…well…

Now what?

Well, everyone does things differently. In years past, when relationships ended in agony, I'd just go out and party until I found a suitable male proxy I cared less about. I thought, now that I'm twenty-seven and have my shit together (i.e. career, home, friends, stability, cable television and the DVD box set of *Mad Men* Seasons 1-5) it might be time to

---

1   *It's Called a Break-up Because It's Broken: The Smart Girl's Break-up Buddy*, by Greg Behrendt and Amiira Ruotola-Behrendt, 2006. See Appendix A: Things You May Also Like.

try something different.

The most immediate suggestion from everyone was, "Just do online dating."

While not horribly opposed to the ever popular cyber route, I hate that people of my generation proclaim there are *only* two options for a single person: A.) Go to the bar and drink with strangers until you fall into the lap of someone who can tolerate you, or B.) Sign up for an online service which requires completing ridiculously lengthy questionnaires until you find more quality dates with like-minded individuals, who end up tolerating you.

I wanted neither. I wanted a choice C.

I've dated lots before, especially while in college. I used to joke that dating was my Olympic sport. But now, after pouring myself into a relationship I was truly ready to commit to forever, I decided to focus my energies inwardly and not rush to the first penis—I mean opportunity—that came my way.

I didn't want to date anyone. I didn't want to sign up for any website. I didn't want to go out and have meaningless rebound flings. I just wanted to do my own thing again. Be me again, not someone attached to the hip of someone else who after a few years was still allegedly trying to decide whether I was worth his time or not.

Um, fuck that.

Predictably, UPS didn't immediately knock on my door with an emotionally-available Chris Hemsworth look-alike replacement boyfriend. I had to consider other options. No, not girls. I don't think that's really a switch one can purposefully control. I'm not ignorant of the female prospect, but it's never been, how shall I say it, a flavor of ice cream

I've ever found myself wanting to try. However…

Hang on…I'll…

I'll date myself.

That's what I'm going to do.

Behold choice C! Date yourself.

This epiphany became quite a preoccupation. In the months post-break-up my friends and coworkers would say, "Hey, are you seeing anyone yet? I've got someone who might be interested."

My reply became a repeating chorus: "No thanks, I'm dating myself."

It is not necessarily a novel, brilliant idea. People date themselves all the time, i.e. last week when you took a "mental health day" to binge-watch TV for fourteen hours in your sweatpants (*You know nothing, Jon Snow!*). I feel like it is common knowledge that after any type of loss a person should act selfishly in order to heal, but I wasn't going to be so unconvincing. A few days on the couch watching sci-fi movies coupled with one discount spa pedicure wasn't going to cut it. I was going way bigger.

I typed up a "List of Dates" to take myself out on — fifty of them. That's a good number, right? It comprised of things in the city I had wanted to do that I didn't have time for before, places and events to experience, spirits to drink and foods to eat, challenges I didn't have the balls to face, afternoons and evenings to relax and watch the grass grow. Coming up with fifty different ideas proved challenging, and after finishing the List, and printing it out, I looked at it and thought — *Shit, this is gonna be tough.* Even if I did one of these Dates every week it would take me about a year to finish.

I didn't care. It wasn't about the time in which to complete it all. This wasn't a race. There's no crash course for heartbreak, and there wasn't a participation trophy. So why was I doing this?

The alternative was to continue reveling in self-pity, resentment, anger, and extreme unproductiveness, or worse— crawl back to Can't-Make-Up-His-Mind Ex-Boyfriend. In the memorable words of Jennifer Aniston's character Brooke in the movie *The Break-up*—I deserve someone who gives a shit.

No, no, forward was the only direction to go. This was my constructive, unwaveringly bold attempt at jumpstarting myself. This was my new mission.

Anecdotal evidence: My friend Susan (celebrity casting: Susan Sarandon) had gone through a divorce with her husband of twenty-ish years. Their two kids were in college. They sold the house they shared in all that time. She got a place of her own. He did too. They spent time apart trying to put their lives back together. Then one day Susan announced, "Guess what! We're back together!"

Um, what?

Susan explained everything. She spent some time alone, got herself back on her feet, and was feeling whole enough to try dating again. The Fates would have it that she and her now ex-husband signed up for the same online dating service. And they matched with each other. And they went on a date with each other. And she said: "It was a complete new start, like when your computer screen goes blank, you know that Blue Screen of Death, and the only thing you can do is unplug it. Turn it off and turn it on again. That's exactly what it was like. A reboot."

I pondered her words with amazement. They resonated with me profoundly. In all of my girlfriends' lengthy histories with men I had never heard anything like it before. She went on, "I'm so deliriously happy, and I wish this happiness for each of you," pointing to the rest of our group of friends.

Now, my own personal rebooting will definitely not include a similar reunion with Dufus. Sorry, spoiler alert.

To add to the initial disclaimers, this is not a self-help book. I am not telling you to do this to get over your break-up, or whatever else you are going through. I'm not a counselor, relationship expert, life coach, psychotherapist, psychiatrist, palm reader, or other type of medium. I am, however, a recently-heartbroken full-time-working registered nurse a few years shy of thirty, whose top qualities include a flair for story-telling, beer-drinking, and shenanigan-seeking in and around Portland, Oregon's quirky present-day single scene.

Honestly, I'm simply a person logging my attempt at trying something new. This is what I did and how I did it, and why I did it. You may decide this is a stupid idea. You may decide to do something similar or completely different. You might make a list of fifty different mountains to climb, fifty different gourmet cheeseburgers to consume, or fifty dates with fifty different people of your preferred gender(s). In any case, I hope you have health insurance.

Further warnings: Sometimes I swear. Sometimes I delve into the intimate parts of my life or others. I'd say this narrative is somewhere between PG-13 and definitely don't read aloud to conservative Grandma. Sometimes I hyperbolize but it's my account, not someone else's to fact check; I swear these things really happened. I couldn't make this shit up if I tried. I've changed people's names to protect their anonymity/sanity, but also because it is super hilarious to typecast friends, family, and strangers into celebrity molds.

I might have an IMDB.com problem.

You might be reading this because you know me and saw my List of Dates and want to see how it all played out. You might be reading this because you broke up with someone and you are also wondering how to get yourself off the couch (Step one, get off the couch). You might be reading this because I need someone to edit, or you might be my mom.

The point is this is the story of my Reboot. I went on fifty Dates with myself. Some of them were so successful I continue to repeat them; others made for one-time-only specials. I hope it reads as a mix between a blog of bonafide self-indulgence and a journal of new adventures in the uncertain realm of being single and unattached, sprinkled with side stories of inappropriate hilarity.

I sincerely hope you enjoy hearing about it at least half as much as I enjoyed living it.

Marie MacMillan

50 Dates with Myself

1. See a play at a theater I haven't been to yet
2. Attend OMSI After Dark
3. Make a meal entirely from Farmer's Market purchases
4. Participate in a hiking group
5. Go river rafting or kayaking
6. Take a tai chi class
7. Timbers Army volunteer event
8. Visit the Oregon History Museum
9. Geek Trivia Night at Kennedy School
10. See an indie film at NW Film Center
11. Take a cooking class
12. Go on a bike ride (aka. Confront your fear of biking!)
13. Spa Day…seriously, spend most of the day there.
14. Visit the Grotto
15. Visit a new exhibit at the Portland Art Museum
16. Sign up for an open mic night somewhere
17. Tour Pioneer Courthouse
18. Attend a Wednesday Free Concert at the Old Church

19. Go to Portland Meadows (Opening Day is Sunday October 12)
20. Go to a comedy show
21. Enter a contest
22. See a classical music performance
23. Attend a McMenamins history night
24. See something at Roseland Theater
25. Go on a walking tour somewhere
26. Find a meet-the-chef dinner
27. Take a new dance class
28. Take a yoga class
29. Audition for something!
30. Attend the Portland Opera
31. Take an art class, or finish an art project already in process. Spend at least half a day on it.
32. Go to a Fashion Week event
33. Attend a festival you haven't been to
34. Attend an author reading
35. Go to a wine tasting
36. Go to a University Sporting event
37. Tour a brewery you haven't toured yet
38. Manicure/Pedicure just because. Not because you have a date or an event or a trip. Just fucking because.
39. Take yourself out to lunch at a restaurant you haven't been to
40. Spend an afternoon or evening just reading a novel, drinking wine.
41. Try a new sport
42. After renewing your lease, buy something new for the apartment. Something solid.

43. Sell some books at Powell's, then buy a new book worth having. Lunch at Boxer Ramen.
44. Sell some clothes at Buffalo Exchange, then buy a new article of clothing worth having. Lunch at new place.
45. Do something scary. Scarier than your normal every-day scary.
46. Take a solo road trip. Must be gone from home at least the whole day.
47. Picnic solo. Park of choice.
48. Go to an event that requires singing. (In the shower does not count.)
49. Volunteer for kids somewhere doing something productive.
50. Put on a dress. Take out some friends. Buy them drinks. Have a great night. Then frame this epic list, because congratulations, you are a certified badass.

Part 1

The first thirteen Dates

"I think you are wrong to want a heart. It makes most
people unhappy.
If you only knew it, you are in luck not to have a heart."

— Oz to the Tin Woodman, *The Wonderful Wizard of Oz*,
Chapter 15, by L. Frank Baum

August 14th 2014 — Break-ups often turn people to extremes. Extreme drinking, extreme eating, extreme fasting, extreme name calling, extreme pouting, extreme gym/tan/laundry-ing, whatever fits your fancy. Eating is not my forte when I'm heartbroken.

Currently, I forget breakfast and don't eat until 2pm. Food does not interest me. At least real food; instant Kraft Mac & Cheese does not count no matter how much I try to convince myself.

Today is officially two weeks post break-up and no different. I've had one cup of day-old coffee and half a cup of instant oatmeal. I put tea bags on my eyes for a few minutes to minimize swelling, a feeble attempt at destroying the evidence of my nighttime sobbing. I don't want to eat. I don't want to do anything. However, I do need to take in real calories and protein today since I have a long work meeting, which brings me to crossing off the first of fifty Dates with myself.

No. 39
Take yourself out to lunch at a restaurant you haven't been to.

I suppose this is one of the easiest, for obvious reasons. According to the social media masses, it was the second annual Portland Burger Week, or #pdxburgerweek, during which several restaurants participate by offering $5 burgers. I had a 1 p.m. hospital committee meeting, so I took myself to the bar/eatery attached to the famed Mississippi Studios in North Portland, astutely named Bar Bar. I ordered the $5 burger special, a side of onion rings, and found my way outside to the patio. I filled my red plastic cup of water and delved into the most recent *Eleven* publication available at the front.

I had one hour to myself. To eat lunch. In said eatery I hadn't had the opportunity to visit yet.

Ho, hum.

I spent an hour eating 94% of the gigantic burger, thumbing through the zine pages casually, and checking my phone aimlessly about every six minutes like every other single person who eats alone in public at 11:55 a.m. on a weekday.

I looked for the help-yourself water station as I needed a refill. An entire construction crew of sweaty men stopped in to avail themselves of the $5 burger offer, and I would literally have to step over their muddy jeans to get myself more water. Damn you, sodium-filled onion ring batter. I was in a cute sundress on my first official Date out with myself and I didn't want to invite other dudes or eyes or inquiries. Five-years-ago-Marie would have relished this opportunity; however, I skipped the refill. I forbid myself from even thinking about flirting with available dudes until I'm done with this fifty-Date challenge.[2] I quickly finished the contents of my burger basket and headed to my five-and-a-half hour face-palm, I mean work meeting.

For a first Date, it wasn't spectacular. I couldn't really be myself. I couldn't even get up to get more water. There was no wait staff. I'm not sure if it really counted for "taking myself out to lunch." In fact, I think the real Date[3] happened later that night when I was in my pajamas, after I cooked myself a nice dinner, lit a candle, and drank two glasses of $6.99 Malbec while laughing at Cameron Diaz joke around in *The Other Woman*. I thought the trailer was better than the movie, but I'm glad I spent $5.99 on it. I cried at the end, but then again, I cry a lot these days. That was the real Date. Though, I think by eating in public, at an establishment yet to happily take my cash, in a sundress no less, this fulfils the requirements stated in No. 39. At least, it led me to an evening where I went to bed feeling incrementally, infinitesimally, and ever-so-slightly less shitty than I did the day before.

August 18, 2014—It was another summer day off and my social calendar was wide open. The predicted high temperature was 91 degrees Fahrenheit. I needed to get out of my hot apartment.

---

2   This does not last.

3   Date = an outing with myself which applies to one of the 50 on the List
   date = an outing with another individual for potential romantic purposes,
or a specific box on the calendar

No. 47
Picnic solo. Park of choice.

I packed up some lingering refrigerator inhabitants in Tupperware: grilled chicken strips, avocado, lettuce, and deli salad. I put the food along with a cloth napkin, a plate, a knife and fork in an actual wicker picnic basket found in my grandmother's basement. In one of my many large canvas bags I rolled up a blanket, sunscreen, a magazine, my e-reader, a book, headphones, and a water bottle. If I'm going to picnic I better do it right—although I did skip the wine and wine glass, thinking 11:25 a.m. was probably too early…probably.

I took my basket, which looks like it belongs to Dorothy in the *Wizard of Oz*, and walked downtown. I first stopped at Pioneer Square for their Monday afternoon Farmer's Market. Read: Farmer's Markets are to Portland as taxi cabs are to New York City.

Okay, possibly hyperbole, but not far off.

This was a smaller market, but I needed something sweet for my picnic. I purchased an orange-chocolate muffin from an independent bakery stand. Then, I made my way to Tom McCall Waterfront Park, five blocks east on the bank of the Willamette River. The park is close to home and it is the most saturated with people for good people-watching.

I waded through the runners, hula-hoopers, skateboarders, hula-hoopers on skateboards, vagrants, strollers and mommies, cyclists, the Darth Vadar bag-piping unicyclist[4], and chose

---

4   aka "the Unipiper." Contentious among the greater local bag-piping community. https://bit.ly/VSSRDm

a shaded spot underneath a tree near the wharf with the sailboats. Funny enough, this part was pretty secluded. Most of the people milled about near the old piers just off the running path. I sat way up on the hill, away from as much goose poop and/or human poop as possible.

I finished my lunch without much enjoyment. I watched the sailboats sit stagnantly and a few kayakers stream by (reminded myself to get researching for No. 5).

I ate. The world went by.

Well…that's that, I thought. No fireworks or internal epiphanies.

I picked up my ancient picnic basket and walked back through the hordes of park-goers, crossed over to the train, and took it back to my end of downtown. I resituated my blanket and literary camp in the Park Blocks[5] near Portland State University. It wasn't quite as ostentatious or populous as the Waterfront, but it had enough passersby to help me not publicly cry my way through *It's Called a Break-up Because It's Broken* and *The Single Woman's Sassy Survival Guide*—the two self-help books Amazon recommended for me based on my recent internet searches. Yeesh.

I finished Mandy Hale's *Survival Guide* in one sitting— encouraging and worthwhile, for those of you needing emotional validation. I was on Chapter 2 of Greg Behnrendt and Amiira Ruotola-Behnrendt's *Broken* when I decided to eat my farmer's market dessert muffin. However, to my utter dismay, the frosted chocolate topping of my muffin was stuck to the paper sack the nice bakery lady put it in. I realized the delicate situation and tried carefully to peel

---

5   Blocks throughout downtown with green spaces in-between the large buildings. https://bit.ly/2ksP2aG

off the paper stuck to my dessert. Despite my efforts, all the chocolate icing came off with the paper.

My muffin was now chocolate-less.

Like my life.

I felt like the kid whose ice-cream scoop fell off the cone into the dirt. Just as I was about to give in to my sadness and weep into the grass, my good friend Blake (celebrity casting choice: Blake Lively) texted me offering an emotional escape: "Hey I'm tired of my office. Wanna go to Sauvie Island?"

Yuh-duh-duh-DAH. BFF to the Rescue!

Blake has been my cheerleader and single-life superhero over the first two weeks post-break-up (and let's be honest, the two months of awful pre-break-up debate). She is the encouraging, tell-it-like-it-is buddy that all broken-hearted people need in their lives.

Not wanting to wallow in sadness under the Park Block trees anymore, I packed up my picnic camp and headed home, put on my swimsuit, picked up Blake and headed out on the highway.

We had a fun time on the sandy beach of the river island, catching up on the weekend's latest, drinking Strongbow cider and people watching. It was an escape indeed, actual physical distance from the city—aka the place where I spent the last two years dating Dufus. Again, the Date listed was mediocre compared to the activity it led to.

I snuggled into bed (after moving the tortilla chip bags and tissue boxes) feeling like goodness had won over evil, superhero style—my Blake Lively best friend in a cape swatting away ghouls of breakup badness.

Evaluating the two Reboot experiences thus far, I would have to say the lesson I've learned while enduring the one-month post-break-up window is this: Spend the majority of your time with people who are positive influences in your life. In fact, saturate your social calendar. Keep busy. You have plenty of time to sleep alone during the night hours to overthink the weepy upheaval, download self-help books, and try unsuccessfully to ignore the gigantic hole in your chest cavity.

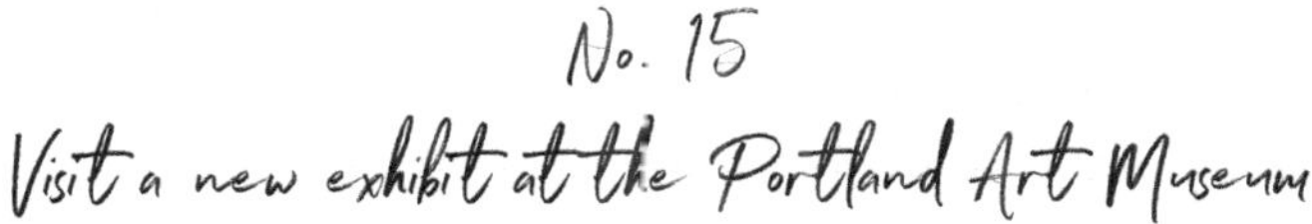

August 20th 2014—My good friend from work Cate (celebrity casting: Cate Blanchett) has gone through a similar loss in her life. She and a platonic friend have gone through a break-up. Cate has never been involved in a romantic relationship, as she will readily admit, so this pretty much has had an equivalent effect on her, i.e. she also has a hole in her chest cavity, and like me she is trying to fill it with healthy distractions.[6] Before I could stop her from doing so, Cate temporarily stole my printed List of Dates and made a photocopy for herself. She then highlighted those she wanted to try. I made her swear not to make any more copies for fear someone at work might think I'm insane.

Cate noted the Portland Art Museum visit on the List. She planned to go see the new exhibit and invited me. I originally thought I'd do all 50 Dates by myself, but I realized that would be near impossible. Also, echoing the sentiment of "spend time with positive influences on your

---

6   As opposed to unhealthy distractions like drinking alone in strange bars, going home with strange guys, and ending up with strange diagnoses from your gynecologist.

life," it gave me a chance to stop binge-watching terrible reality shows and get off the couch. And put on a bra…and pants, for God's sake.

Adjectives I'd use to describe Cate: intentional, inquisitive, and thoughtful. She's a thirty-eight-year-old pharmacist and spends her well-earned cash on five-star trips around the globe. We met at the museum to experience the current exhibit: *The Art of the Lourve's Tuileries Garden*. It was bright and airy, like being at a garden party. The paintings were lovely, the statues dominating but in a soft way. The video media, a short film of conglomerated footage taken at the famed gardens displayed on three flat walls via projector on loop, was the cherry on top of the French-vanilla sundae.

That's right. I'm a cultured hippie-citizen primed for *Portlandia* sketch comedy. I'm not knowledgeable enough to describe brush strokes or cast-iron techniques but I can appreciate most art forms. Anyhow, we spent a good hour and half immersing ourselves in the francophilia. Then, we visited the farmer's market going on right outside in the Park Blocks. This one used to be pretty small, but now it's gigantic. The focus on produce stands is freaking spectacular. I mean, how many places in America can you get a hot vegan crepe along with your already purchased okra, shiitake mushrooms, eggplant, marionberries, and peppers of every color? The taxicab analogy is not far off. Need I say more on the farmer's markets front? We'll talk more when I get to No. 3.

Anyhow, we skipped the vegan crepes and opted for lunch at my favorite sushi place. We dished briefly on our respective heartbreak dealings and how we were coping. Cate did the requisite social media post on her amazing food excursions; actually she photographed my sashimi plate.

It was a nice afternoon. My feelings were validated by a good friend. I immersed myself in art and community. I felt like I was on track to getting better, as if heartbreak is a terrible viral infection and my only option was to nurse myself back to health. No magic antibiotics for me.

Side Story #1
Hitting Rock Bottom and the Infamous Possession Exchange

There is a dive bar around the corner from my building. It would take probably fifty steps to get from my front door to its grimy threshold. As far as dive bars go, it's an excellent specimen. It is the basement of a crappy hotel chain, so naturally the smell of cigarettes, sour milk, and shame will never fully escape its walls. It has all the glorious characteristics of what makes a dive bar a dive bar, including but certainly not limited to: mostly indigestible food, extremely stiff drinks, a variety of regulars, karaoke five nights a week, tables outside, tables inside, sports fans, pool players, cross-dressers, roller derby girls with tattoos, nerdy boys with laptops, beards galore, loosened ties, trashy tank tops, and enough alcohol and dim lighting to never let any patron feel embarrassed about anything at all. Its occupancy is never ever 100% empty and never ever 100% full.

Needless to say, The Corner Bar is and has been since I moved in to my apartment one of my favorite places, although I haven't frequented it as much as say the other pubs downtown. It's not my first go-to[7], but it's convenient. So this convenience, along with the magnificent description above, makes a near lethal combination for broken-hearted-me living within direct eyesight of its messy splendor.

Well, between the last Date with myself and the next, I dove into my personal tragedy. I suspect that's partly why they are called dive bars; people cope with their personal lives by diving into alcohol. According to Wikipedia, a 1961 dictionary defined a dive bar as "a disreputable resort for drinking or entertainment," aka my kind of party at the time.

One evening Blake wanted to get drinks "somewhere casual" so I suggested the walking-distance watering hole; that way I wouldn't care about not washing my puffy-eyed face and it was T-shirt and jeans acceptable. When Blake showed up I was already working on a gin-and-tonic and a beer, in old jeans and a disheveled *Return of the Jedi* T-shirt. She laughed at my demeanor and ordered. After two drinks she left me there to my own shenanigans.

My mother (celebrity casting: Sally Field) might read this book, so I'll spare the boring details of the night's events. I'm sure you can put the puzzle pieces together. I closed the bar with a few other drinkers. I went home alone, to someone's disappointment. I spent an hour in my bathroom physically recalling the drinks of the last few hours, and I slept poorly. The next day was painful; however, I truly needed to get hitting rock bottom out of my system.

Yes, that's right—I view my bottom of the ocean moment as productive. I needed to get the "*Why? Why? Why, God, why?!*" out of my head, and I did so in brilliantly drunken

____

7   This changes as time goes on. The Corner Bar becomes my several-days-a-week go-to right around 25/50 Dates.

fashion, and while my mind felt lighter my brain felt like it was in a pressure cooker. Nowhere to go but up from here.

During my hangover recovery, Dufus texted me wanting to meet up, to exchange the remnants of possessions we had at each other's places. As if I hadn't done enough damage to myself in the last twenty-four hours already, I agreed.

I just wanted to get it over with. I didn't want any more excuses for him to message me or visit or contact me until I stopped caring so damn much about him. All I had left of his belongings were sweatpants and a T-shirt he slept in. His toiletries I tossed…out my window.

We met in front of his building like we had hundreds of times before. Living eight blocks apart I usually walked but this time I drove. I wanted to look like I was on my way somewhere and just fitting this into my busy schedule. That and I wanted a rapid escape route. Oh yeah, I put on makeup and a dress and made my hair look nice. No woman sees an ex on purpose looking gross, if she can help it.

Dufus sauntered down to my car where I was leaning against my driver door. I hadn't seen him in weeks. I handed him his pajamas back and he handed me a paper bag with an iron that I lent him, and…*drum roll please*…an empty picture frame that once held a 5x7 photo of us.

Wow. What a dick.

"What, did you toss the picture?" I asked, stymied, holding the empty silver frame.

"No, I kept it. It's somewhere else," Dufus replied. "I thought you'd use the picture frame before I did."

Yeah, I'll put a picture of me and my new, better, hotter, more emotionally available boyfriend in it.

I don't want to waste precious time explaining about

how OCD and annoyingly particular Dufus is, but ~~most~~ ~~women~~ most people would interpret this empty picture frame gesture as: *I'm happy to rid you from my life.* Knowing him, I knew it was likely more: *This picture frame does not fit in the carefully arranged pristine condition of my high-rise condo that I never let anyone into. Also it reminds me of you.*

Either way, IT FELT FUCKING TERRIBLE.

After a few brief minutes of polite conversation about work, life, and shit I didn't want to care about anymore, Dufus asked me: "So, how's your mom? She hate me?"

"You know, I gotta go," I stammered. I hit my limit.

"Don't you wanna grab dinner or something? Why did you drive?" Dufus added. Was he kidding?

"No I have plans, I gotta go," I replied. Panic and tears were starting to set in.

"Babe, come on, we still care about each other…" Dufus muttered, shuffling his feet. The wetness escaped my eyelids.

Get out. Get out now. Eject the cockpit! Pull the parachute!

"I gotta go," I said, opening my car door. It was the only thing I could say. I was physically incapable of uttering anything else. Maybe it was the hangover affecting my voice at the time, or maybe I just knew it wouldn't make a difference if I said anything else at all.

"Okay, well, can I get a friendly hug at least?"

My reply was a *you've-gotta-be-kidding* laugh as I wiped my eyes.

"Okay, you're right, we shouldn't," he said, downtrodden. Maybe it was sinking in for him, finally.

I smiled as best I could and we waved at each other somberly while I pulled away and drove in any opposite direction as fast as my car could take me. I somehow ended up at Fred Meyer[8] where I bought Gatorade (still nursing the hangover), magazines, and at least $60 of new makeup. I'm sure I looked pretty pathetic hiccupping over juicy sobs while reading mascara descriptions.

When I got home I was overcome with my inability to distract myself from staring at THAT EMPTY FUCKING PICTURE FRAME, its pretty silver outline shining against the vacant, brown cardboard inset—going over and over in my head what I would've said to Dufus had I the ability to speak.

I had purged my apartment of all things Dufus-related already. Photos were in a taped-shut shoebox. I tossed the empty silver frame into a collection of other newly empty frames stacked in a corner; all previously held photos of us together. I imagined handing him the pile of empty picture frames from my apartment. I would be handing him about six or seven, whereas he gave me just the one. I guess that was the crux of it.

I immediately stopped playing with the new makeup and magazines and sat down at my laptop. I wrote out one single-page document. I typed out everything I wanted to say to him after he stupidly said, *Babe, we still care about each other*. I can't recall exactly what I wrote. I know I didn't allow myself to edit so it was everything I wanted to say/scream at him. Even if I did say all of those calculated and unfiltered sentiments to him in the heat of the moment it would make no difference to our relationship that was, and is, very much over.

I printed out the solitary page. I did not save the file. I took the paper out to my sun room and opened all the windows.

---

8   A grocery store chain in the Pacific Northwest

I read the page aloud to myself. Once. (Okay, twice.)

Then I lit the son-of-a-bitch on fire and let it burn in an aluminum pie tin, along with every feeling in me that wanted to hang on to him, our relationship, and the future I wanted but now wouldn't and shouldn't have.

A brief moment of catharsis followed.

And then to my complete astonishment, my open-air sunroom let the immediate neighborhood know that it has a perfect in-working-order smoke alarm.

August 26th 2014—I woke up after sleeping in, wondering what to do on my day off.[9] I sat in bed curled up in my pajamas messing around on my phone aimlessly. I checked today's high temperature: 93 degrees. Ugh, got to get out of the brick building again. Put clothes on. Stop binge-watching *Star Trek: The Next Generation* (you've seen every episode multiple times, Marie) and walk around like a normal person, not a heartless zombie.

If you learn anything about native Portlanders[10], when there's sunshine and good weather we go absolutely nuts. I find Pacific Northwesterners in general to be very *carpe diem* when it comes to summer. So I figure it's the end of August and I have limited opportunity to check off a few of the outdoor options on my List of 50 Dates. Behold, Google provided me with Portland Kayak Company, which launches

---

9   Future me is re-reading this sentence laughing. Ah to be twenty-seven, single, and without many obligations. But to clarify for the readers, at the time I was working three twelve-hour hospital shifts a week 7:00 a.m. -7:30 p.m. on a variable schedule. I would have strings of days off to Date myself. You like the sound of this? Check out nursing school.

10   Anyone who has lived in the city long enough to remember 45-degree rain every June, pre-global warming consensus.

three-hour tours from the South Waterfront Marina on the Willamette River.

No. 5
Go river rafting or kayaking

I called; I signed up; I got out of bed. Success already.

To sum up: kayaking was freaking awesome. I had no idea this much fun (sans beer) was less than a mile from my house. I had been kayaking once before near the San Juan Islands, in a two-person tandem with Dufus. I had been white water river-rafting a few times. I hadn't tried kayaking in a boat all to myself.

I found it not as difficult as I imagined. After a brief get-to-know-the-kayak in the marina, a group of eight plus a guide headed out onto the slow and flat Willamette River with the simple goal of rounding Ross Island and coming back.

The day was hot and sunny, the guide was super helpful, and we got beautiful views of our tiny cute cityscape. Lots of people were on the water with other types of watercraft. Many times, our twenty-two-year-old guide saw her friends and colleagues jetting or paddling around. She said she rows crew for Lewis and Clark College, is starting her junior year and plans to spend the first semester studying abroad in Ireland.

True, twenty-two was only five years ago for me, but damn, when I think about all the things that have happened in that half decade, I am amazed at how much I've grown—how many guys I've dated, how many places I've lived, how I've progressed in my career, how proud I am of myself for kicking a definitely-not-going-anywhere relationship to the curb. I got nostalgic paddling along in my lengthy orange kayak. I found it easy to relax and watch the water go by, and let my mind wash over beneficial things.

I imagined having this conversation with myself at age thirty-two, five years from now. Surely, I'll have grown even more in that time period. I wonder about the things I'll experience, the places I'll go, the guy(s) I'll date—*how many more times I'll go kayaking.* This was addictive. I have to do this more.

"You know, the company takes tours to Baja, Mexico in the fall and spring. It's four or eight days and you paddle around an island and camp, snorkel, hike, whatever," the guide tells me.

Oh my God, I'm going.

I started Googling kayaking classes and reading the company website as soon as I got home, more ideas for No. 45 and No. 46.

September 2nd, 2014—Labor Day Weekend came and went without much fanfare. I had the day off. Originally, it was going to be my summer holiday to work, but somehow too many people signed up and I got bumped off the schedule. Two months ago I would have been ecstatic about this…but that was two months ago.

I ended up going to my parents' house and hanging out with the family on the deck; playing with my niece and nephew, eating pasta, drinking beer, chatting animatedly with my brothers Topher (celebrity casting: Topher Grace) and Andy (Andy Samberg). I think I did a good job of hiding the fact that I wished Dufus were there—not in his current capacity, obviously, but in every capacity I wanted him to be.

One of the sage/pathetic self-help-post-break-up books I've been reading has a good point: No matter how great someone's potential is you have to date their reality.

My Labor Day reality didn't coincide with Dufus's reality—past, present, or future.

Along with the everyday existential crises that accompany my hospital work life, accepting the above as fact was weighing heavily on my psyche. My next day off I decided to find spiritual relief.

No. 14
Visit the Grotto

The Grotto, or more officially the National Sanctuary of Our Sorrowful Mother, is a ninety-year-old Catholic site of adoration. Specifically, an altar hewn from the face of Rocky Butte features a replica of Michelangelo's famed sculpture *Pietà*. Atop the dormant volcano is a moderately-sized garden around the Servite residence that includes not only beautiful flora, but also a tiny chapel to St. Anne, a meditation chapel overlooking the northern border of the state and the Columbia River, and various other mini-altars and symbols.

Congruent with church tradition, it costs $5 to take the elevator to the top. Insert eye roll here. If I didn't self-identify as Catholic, I would consider it simply a tourist spot with an outdoor church. However, I was raised in the Roman tradition and ergo have to have more respect for it than that.

My also-single Catholic aunt, Melissa (celebrity casting choice: Melissa McCarthy), and I had been meaning to get together to catch up. As a devout person herself I thought she'd like this number on my List. After lunching together, we drove over. We had chosen a beautiful, sunny day to walk around outside the Grotto gardens, admire the various multi-cultural altars, and compare the power and plights of our singledom, despite being twenty-five years apart in age, and then at times not talk at all, just stare at all the Grotto had to offer.[11]

It was nice to be able to be quiet.

I apologize to the reader, I'm about to get preachy. Forgive the small soapbox, I'm not trying to convert anyone, just share my experience.

For those of you not aligned with any type or organized religion, or even those of you who claim zero spirituality of any kind, I can't say anything else other than as a human being with a troubled heart, it gave me mental and emotional relief to be outside around nature. It brings order to a chaotic mind, and I recommend it.

For those of you familiar with any sort of spiritual tradition, you might appreciate the serenity the familiar structure of an altar, or statue or whatever, can provide the soul. So I recommend it.

For those of you who are Christian, Romans 8:35, 37-39[12]

---

11   https://thegrotto.org/

12   *Who shall separate us from the love of Christ? Shall trouble or hardship or persecution or famine or nakedness or danger or sword?... No, in all these things we are more than conquerors through him who loved us. For I am convinced that neither death nor life, neither angels nor demons, neither the present nor the future, nor any powers, neither height nor depth, nor anything else in all creation, will be able to separate us from the love of God that is in Christ Jesus our Lord.*

has given me comfort lately. I recommend it and the Grotto to any brother or sister in Christ. Don't worry, those weirdo Catholics won't bite you (hard).

For those of you who identify as Roman Catholic (Protestant-biting or not) you might appreciate that I felt able to pray more sincerely standing outside in the sunshine, where it was quiet, without a spoken homily, without monetary offering baskets being passed around, without having to stumble my way through a revised Mass script, without having to do anything but give up my earthly feelings and accept something beyond. And for that, I recommend a visit—to the Grotto if you are nearby, and if you're not, find something like it.

Evening of September 2nd, 2014—That's right, bitches, I got two Dates in one day! I mean they were Dates with myself, so it seems less slutty.

No 27
Take a new dance class.

There is a studio I have wanted to check out. Their studio building was being torn down to construct a brand new one (yes, they have actual money) so their current classes were relocated to the university a few blocks away from me. I paid $15 for a drop-in class—and I kind of wanted my money back at the end!

Sad, right? I mean don't get me wrong, I got a great work

out. I'm just used to classes that focus on choreography and presentation for the majority of the time period. We did warmup and technique for fifty minutes and the instructor spent ten minutes throwing a piece together for the "Advanced/ Beginners Jazz/Lyrical" class-takers.

Advanced/Beginners. What does that even mean? Anyway, I got a good sweat in and I actually felt not-totally-embarrassed walking home in my spandex booty shorts. My legs felt like they looked damn good after a few hundred *battements* and *coupe* turns to Indian drum music.

Was it my imagination or did that guy passing by on his bike almost fall off as he smiled at me?

I am getting the hang of this Dating myself thing. Maybe "advanced/beginner" makes sense after all.

September 7th, 2014 – Last week I had drinks with my girlfriend Emma (celebrity casting: Emma Stone), a defense attorney I met while playing coed flag football several years ago. We still play together from time to time and try to catch up off the field when we can. Adjectives I'd use to describe Emma: loud, purposeful, and loudly purposeful (not necessarily purposefully loud). Emma has the absolute best F-bomb of anyone I've ever known. Ever. It's just perfect. I wish I could capture it in linguistic form. Just the intentional *fffff* then the careless *UUHHHH* followed by the perfect *cccccckkkk*.

Well, I tried.

Anyhow, I was telling her about my List of Dates. I've made it an unconscious habit to use the printed List as a bookmark for whatever I'm reading and therefore am perpetually carrying the List around in my bags. Like Cate, Emma spotted one she could help with.

No. 35
Go to a wine tasting.

Everyone has hobbies, especially single thirty-something professionals without children, but sometimes hobbies evolve into ways of life. Emma tells me after reading the list, "Oh, well I'm taking you wine tasting. I'm a member of three clubs. Are you free next Sunday? Be at my house at 11 a.m."

As if I had no choice and was simply following legal advice, I arrived at her house in Vancouver, Washington at 10:50 a.m. the next Sunday. After a quick tour of her house, and an Instagram of her stripper-shoe-ridden closet, we zoomed in her car (also full of swanky footwear[13]) off to Wine Dispensing Location #1 located in the rural area in and around Battleground, Washington.

Wine Dispensing Location #1 was not open yet.

"Hmm, that's okay, we need provisions," Emma said. We drove to the nearest store, walked into what we thought was Safeway, which turned out to be a Walgreens. We were catching up with each other so intensely I think we forgot to look up at the store sign. We laughed wholeheartedly at this ridiculous mistake while purchasing large bottles of water and several unnecessary bags of candy. We drove back to the now open vineyard and tasting room.

---

13   Clarification: Emma is not and never has been a stripper. She just likes incredibly high heels.

The staff knew her by name. They knew Emma's name at each Wine Dispensing Location we visited that day.

Now, I don't know a lot about wine. I know a lot about beer. I can appreciate the finer details of beer more than the average American adult, and I'd say I'm right on par with the average Portlandian having been to at least 50% of the however many hundred-plus breweries we have per capita now. Let's just say I concluded during my afternoon excursion that the crowd experience from beer to wine didn't easily translate for me.

At our first venue we tasted all they had to offer, plus a seasonal, plus a bottle of what we liked best, and then sat out on the patio eating pizza, salad, and looking out onto the greater sloping hills that meshed into Central Washington Somewhere. By that point Emma's young friend Zach (celebrity casting: Zach Woods) showed up to hang out. I can't say it was her gay friend, but how about the not-certain-about-his-sexuality friend. I know it's not catchy. Anyway, I wasn't the only one who asked that day.

After thoroughly enjoying our Utopian outdoor lunch affair, we saddled off to the next stop, but not before seeing a Yard Sale sign with the subtitled description "GUY STUFF" in large print. Very tipsy Yours Truly thought it would be just excellent to investigate such a claim.

This "YARD SALE: GUY STUFF" sign garnered much laughter and knee-slapping as we turned off the main road to find it. We imagined a woman scorned selling all of her cheating boyfriend's prized possessions.

We couldn't have been more wrong. We followed the signs to a backwoods house far from the main road and found two bearded guys next to an ancient white-haired miser sitting in lawn chairs amongst what appeared to be every piece of outdoor equipment ever invented. The lot was like the remnants of a one-hundred-year-old Home Depot. The two lumberjacks told us their elderly white-haired friend sitting there next to the RV labeled "Will Negotiate" had a recent stroke and can't operate any of his machinery any longer.

Awwww, we said, now feeling like assholes. Emma bought an edger and a hoe which Zach helped load into the car. After all, she had a house and a yard. I couldn't find anything that would remotely help out my downtown living. We wished them the best and headed back out on our wine adventure.

Wine Dispensing Location #2 looked like the Walt Disney World of vineyards. There was, in fact, a wedding going on. The Walt Disney of the vineyard himself, celebrity casting Sean Connery, talked with our trio during our tasting. We went through the selection candidly and Sean Connery practically invited us over to his mansion for dinner, wine in a hot tub if we like—sneaky, dirty old Sean. When we were done with the tasting room, I was drunk enough to take Emma's hand and walk nonchalantly though the wedding reception in progress.

One of the bridesmaids called out, "Carla! Hey Carla!—" waving at someone across the lawn.

"Okay if anyone asks, we are Carla's friends," I said to Emma, sniggering. I thought participating in the reception was a spectacular idea. Emma put her foot down at signing the guest book and hauled me off to her car, giggling all the way.

Wine Dispensing Location #3 was much smaller and rather quiet. By this time in the day I was inundated with words like tannins, cassis, tobacco, fruity, earthy, bold, pungent—*aaagggghhh make it stop.*

I think my taste got as fine as, "I like this," and, "I don't like this."

Emma and I got tacos on the way home and parted ways after polishing off the water bottles and candy. Smart purchases, as it turned out. I slept really, really well. Absolutely fun-filled day. Would do it over again as fast as you can say *full-bodied Syrah.*

I've now had seven Dates with myself. That's about the amount of dates I'd go out with someone before deciding whether he's worth seeing exclusively or not. This is a purely subjective number; for some people it's after three dates, for others it's one. I suppose it depends on how much you like and connect with the other person, and possibly directly proportional to how good the sex is. Well, so far, I think, for an imperfect being, I'm pretty freaking cool. And I already know how sex is with myself, so I say to myself: *Self, I'm having a great time, and I would like to see where this goes.*

No. 43
Sell some books at Powell's then buy a new book worth having. Lunch at Boxer Ramen.

I feel like Portland is one of the few places left in the world that honors the legacy of the independent bookstore. It is impossible for me to visit Powell's Books without spending money. I can never "just look around" without buying something. There's always a kitschy self-published book of poetry, small-press short stories journal, gigantic gardening anthology, or classic sci-fi novel I convince myself I cannot live without. In addition to the quirky awesomeness the independent bookstore provides, author readings help keep the business alive when nowadays it's so easy to click "Purchase" and "Download" from your living room couch. Like many other cool things and places in downtown, Powell's largest store is easily accessed by public transit. Also, it is huge, newly remodeled, and has World Cup Coffee attached to it. Other smaller stores on the West Coast might call the bookstore giant a conglomerated sell-out, but get over yourself Berkeley, California.

Doing all the deep cleaning in my apartment (i.e. de-bugging of Dufus-related materials) I had a stack of books needing to be dealt with. Not that Dufus ever once got me a book, but I had done an up-turning of the apartment, you know the kind you do once a year when you clean the oven, vacuum under the bed, and go through all your clothing thinking, "Will I ever really wear this tank top from 2006 again?" Hence, I had many piles. Piles of books. Piles of clothes. Piles of recycling, garbage, giveaways, and storage. I was physically and metaphorically extricating unnecessary things from my life.

I loaded a canvas bag full of books I pre-checked on the Powell's website confirmed as "sellable." I made silent jokes to myself about the ISBN numbers as I typed them in, reminiscing about how I had to memorize the Dewey Decimal system in elementary school, while kids these days under the age of seven look at a landline telephone and ask what it is. I carried the bag of books via streetcar to Powell's

Books, the flagship store on W. Burnside Street. I sold them for approximately $20 in store credit. Then I spent an hour or so perusing the Blue Room, the gardening section of the Red Room, and the alluring self-publishing kiosk at the entrance to the Purple Room I always take a brochure for but never do anything about. I smiled the whole time; just a smiley nerdy girl reading subtitle after subtitle. I passed similar smiley nerdy people also wearing boots, jeans, and hippie hats. We are Powell's Nation.

I know, I know, I know…cue *Portlandia* sketch.

I ate dinner at Boxer Ramen across the street. I ordered the same ramen noodle bowl I always have. I *slurp, slurp, slurped* as I read the first chapters of *The Kitchen Gardener's Handbook* and wished for a community garden plot.

Zen.

No. 34
Attend an author reading.

Again, initially I thought I wouldn't combine Dates, but hey, I am liking spending time with myself, and in serious relationships dates stretch on for weekends. With the newfound free social calendar why not treat myself to extra Me Time?

After having dinner at Boxer Ramen (I know, not lunch, but whatever) I crossed W. Burnside Street again—ignoring Buffalo Exchange clothing store as much as possible (*YOU HAVE ENOUGH GRAPHIC T-SHIRTS, MARIE*)—entering Powell's Books *again*. I climbed the stairs to the third floor and sat in the front row of chairs set up for the event. The author's reading was sparsely attended, but not without enthusiasm.

The author was a comedian, and this was his witty nonfiction rendition of pop culture satire. Aside from standup, he runs a podcast with guest comedians, and admitted book writing is a new venture. He spent most of the allotted time revealing how the idea for the book came about. I appreciated the story of origin more than the actual read-aloud passages. I found the pop culture references from 1990 and onward moderately humorous, and didn't comprehend anything pre-1985. (Go ahead, make your entitled Millennial comments here.) I'm glad I went, even if it wasn't a groundbreaking experience for me. It gave me insight into book writing, in case this ridiculous retelling of "Dates with Myself" ever makes it off my laptop and into any other form of narration.

Side Story #2
The Rom-Com Theory

(Skype New Conversation Noise)

Me: Hey Wifey!

Julia Stiles *(friend from college)*: Hey, Wifey. How are you doing?

Me: Meh, hangin' in there.

Julia: Have you talked to Dufus at all?

Me: Briefly, when we exchanged possessions.

Julia: Oh. I hate the possession exchange.

Me: He returned an empty picture frame. Like he took the picture of us out and handed me the empty frame.

Julia: What a fucking douchebag. You can
do way better.

Me: Anyway, how's the new apartment?
You and Heath settled in yet?

A Skype tour of Julia's new apartment followed. I waved to her boyfriend. Then a long update of each other's lives, hers in San Luis Obispo as an ecologist dating an optometry student, mine here in Portland as a newly-single nurse. Julia and I were part of an inseparable threesome in college—err, trio of lady friends, totally nonsexual. However, Julia and I call each other Wifey and describe all dealings with men without lack of minor detail.

Julia: So…have you rebounded yet?

Me: Nope. I don't plan to.

Julia: WHAT!?

Me: Yeah, it's just not like other break-ups.
I don't wanna go screw whatever
dick happens to be pointing at me.
I don't wanna date guys at all.

Julia: You wanna date girls?

Me: No, no, no, I've decided to date
myself.

Julia: Interesting…

Me: No, really. I made a list of fifty Dates
to have with myself.

Julia: Ha. Really?

Me: Yeah, like you know, just do stuff I
hadn't done in the city before, things
I've been wanting to try, stuff I didn't
make time for before when I was

pouring blood, sweat, and tears into the relationship with Dufus. So, I wanna do fifty Dates with myself before going on a date with any dude.

Julia: This is amazing. You know what's going to happen though?

Me: What?

Julia: You are gonna meet some guy around Date #35 and he's gonna be all, *Oh, you're amazing, let's get together*, and you're gonna be like, *No, I can't I'm not ready yet*, and he's gonna keep pursuing you and you're gonna start falling for him, and then after Date #50 you guys will get together. You need to blog this thing. Hollywood will eat this shit up.

Me: You think so huh?

Julia: Are you kidding? It's totally romantic comedy quality.

Me: Huh. Okay. I know who'll play you in the movie.

Julia: Who?

Me: That girl who plays the cute funny slutty friend in all the romantic comedies. Hang on, I'm IMDB-ing her.

Julia: Which girl?

Me: Judy Greer.

Julia: Wait…(*looking online*) Oh, noooooo. No, Julia Stiles would definitely play me.

Me: Okay, Julia Stiles. And your boyfriend
        is Heath Ledger.

Julie: Score.

Me: But really you're the hot female
        version of Jonah Hill.

Julia: Right. Who will play the guy who
        sweeps you off your feet?

Me: Hmmm Chris Platt. Chris Hemsworth.
        Chris Pine.

Julia: Wait, who?

Me: You know, any of the hot Hollywood
        Chrises.

Julia: Riiiiiight. I know who will play you.

Me: Who will play me?

Julia: Elliot Page.

Me: A tall Elliot Page.

September 10th, 2014—Another day off work, another opportunity to greet the world with unattached singular charm. Hey, I do earn income, I swear. Thirty-six hours per week at the hospital is full time work. I promise I am not a secretly wealthy foreign princess who can't make love work.

No. 3
Make a meal entirely from Farmer's Market purchases.

I did not grow up cooking or preparing food for myself, other than a bowl of cereal before school. Meal-prepping skills in my semi-adulthood consisted mostly of "Just Add ___" dinner boxes and throwing together salads (see No. 11). I wanted to get better at cooking for myself so this struck me as a fun, earth-friendly way.

In the waning summer sun, I walked through the farmer's market in Shemanski Park[14] with a giant canvas bag and one mission, as stated above.

Translation: act as pretentiously as possible.

Not just New Seasons organic grocery[15] level of pretentious, I'm talking neighborhood co-op produce store where the cashiers are rotating volunteers with dread-locks who try to sell you homemade lemongrass lip balm and biodegradable dishwashing liquid, pretentious.

My farmer's market purchases included cipollini onions, a bunch of carrots, zucchini, cherry tomatoes, butter lettuce, a quart of raspberries, possibly-pasteurized herb goat cheese spread, and a white bread baguette. And, because I'm not into the vegan thing, I picked up the largest piece of protein available, a hunk of wild-caught salmon.

I took my raw materials with me to the next phase of the day.

---

14   The same farmer's market outside of The Portland Art Museum I walked through with Cate in No. 15

15   Spendy and popular organic grocery chain based in Portland

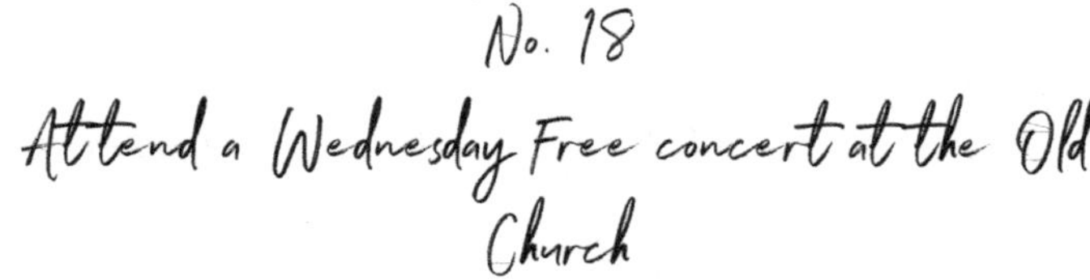

I walked from Shemanski Park to The Old Church[16]—really, that is its actual name.

The Old Church (not the building, the society that maintains it) puts on Free Sack Lunch concerts every Wednesday. The Old Church (the building itself) had its first cornerstone laid in 1882. The original pipe organ was a gift from prominent 19th century Portland family, the Ladds.[17] It sounds so heavenly, tiny cherubs fly out of the pipes and shoot you with arrows of religious guilt.[18]

I'm 88% sure I was the youngest person at the concert, mostly because I think I was the only one to walk into the building through the main doors and not through the wheelchair entrance with a walker. I read the program feeling slightly out of place as senior day-trip groups seated themselves. Slowly. With lots of creaking from both the building's scaffolding and the elderly's bone joints.

What followed was a lovely, professional one-hour concert, a classical duet; a semi-renowned pianist and an organist playing a concerto. I stared out the stained-glass window, glancing between my List of Dates and recipes on my phone. Walking home with my canvas bag, carrot spouts bouncing out the top, I looked and felt as pretentous

---

16   https://theoldchurch.org/

17   True

18   False

as I expected.

To finish off No. 3, I upped the hipster level when I got to the meal cooking part. Originally, I planned to use *only* the ingredients from the market, but I wanted the meal to be edible. So, I used my own spices and olive oil and added a side of instant rice, but those were the only additives. Hey, I did my best. I baked the salmon with the veggies. I spread the goat cheese on the baguette and topped it with freshly mashed raspberry.

That's right. I spread *mother-fucking goat cheese* on a *mother-fucking baguette.*

Mission accomplished, and it all tasted damn delicious.

However, most unfortunately, the worst case of gastroenteritis I have ever suffered followed shortly after.

I'd like my organic vegetables[19] with a side of pesticides from now on.

No. 7
Timbers Army volunteer event.

September 13th 2014—Someone, surely, has or is in the process of writing a comprehensive narrative on the history of the Timbers Army.[20] For the anti-sports readers out there, I'll do my best to be brief.

The Portland Timbers is a soccer club that started in Portland in 1975. It has been resurrected from defunct leagues to minor leagues, and elevated from minor leagues to now

---

19   Looking back, I don't remember putting that unrefrigerated salmon on ice in-between the market trip, the one-hour concert, and cooking at home. What an inexperienced kid I was! Ouch.

20   https://timbersarmy.org/aboutus/history

Major League Soccer. The modest yet striking stadium sitting in the bottom of Goose Hollow neighborhood has evolved in attendance and name: from filling Civic Stadium in the late 1970s, to sparse attendance in PGE Park in the '90s, to standing room only Jeld-Wen Field circa 2011, to overflowing 22,000 seats in the latest-named Providence Park this summer of 2014. It has gone from something big, to something forgotten, to ten guys with beers banging on garbage cans, to sold-out matches where one-thousand strong wave flags and chant loudly for ninety-plus minutes—the Timbers Army (TA).

I know I must overly romanticize it, as a supporter how can I not—sorry if you are a Seattle Sounders fan[21]—but even if you hate soccer and love other sports this is a must-see event. Oh yeah, and there is (debatably) professional soccer to watch, too.

Somewhat unexpectedly, the TA herself has evolved equally. While its primary purpose is obsessive communal cheerleading on an enormous scale, it has bled into philanthropic realms with community CPR classes, rebuilding outdated city soccer fields, scholarships to local and Third World players, a playground for disabled children, the list goes on. As a season ticket holder and member of this quirky soccer community officially dubbed the 107ist, it is easy for me to elucidate how game day is a glorious sight to behold but I am particularly proud of what the TA organization has become.

But getting back to my List—I wanted to pepper in good-doing with my Dates of selfishness. Enrich others' lives and you enrich your own, right? Point being, since I am already a member of this monstrous charitable sporting society, the

---

21   Actually no, I'm not sorry. Fuck Seattle.

good-doing was easily accessible and I needed to tap into it.

The North American soccer season was nearing its end by September so the opportunities for volunteer events were getting limited. On this night, the TA decided to throw itself a Block Party in front of the Fanladen[22] with kegs of beer, bounce houses for kids, and giant screens to show the away game on television. With idiotic passion, a few hundred supporters were chanting at relatively small televisions hoisted up on platforms, and chugging homebrews while their kids ran around. I walked up to this familiar scene as the game was ending. I changed into jeans as soon as I got off shift so I was ready for volunteer clean-up crew. I said hello to Blake and her new boyfriend Jake (celebrity casting: Jake Johnson), drank a beer, and then the game was over. We lost, people vacated the premises, and I began helping dump ice into the gutters, haul trash bags to corners, and whatever else people in charge needed.

I think I helped for a total of twenty minutes. Because of the super powers the TA holds, with about fifty people we had the street cleaned up and fanfare packed away in that short amount of time. I don't remember being surprised.

Well it wasn't the volunteer experience I had hoped for, but it counts. I guess I'll have to make up for the good-doing factor with No. 49.

---

22   German. Fan hangout/clubhouse, epicenter of TA operations

Side Story #3
The Brokenness

Dufus and I did a lot together; we traveled, we camped, we went to sporting events, we went to breweries, we stayed in and watched TV shows while I made brunch and he cleaned my kitchen to perfection. We did many things just the two of us, but Dufus had two close friends, Jeremy (celebrity casting: Jeremy Renner) and Ken (celebrity casting: Ken Jeong) who we hung out with pretty regularly. Jeremy was married and Ken had a girlfriend, and the six of us became a traveling Circus of Fun.

Like I mentioned before in the Prologue, Dufus and I had this flirtatious friendship go on for two years before he asked me out on a legitimate date. This first date happened to be Jeremy's marriage to Rooney (celebrity casting: Rooney Mara). In typical last-minute non-committal Dufus fashion, he asked me the night before the wedding if I'd be his plus-one. Like the badass I was, I already had a date planned with a different guy, but I cancelled it (along with my commitments to indoor soccer and flag football teams) to go the wedding with Dufus. I specifically and vividly remember thinking, already totally enamored with him: *I will regret it the rest of my life if I don't say yes and go on this date.*

Fast forward two-and-a-half years: Jeremy and Rooney have a nice house and both have new jobs. Ken and his girlfriend Lisa (celebrity casting: Lisa Kudrow) have moved in together into Ken's house. And Dufus and I have broken up, not surprising to anyone in the Circus of Fun who knew us better as a couple than most. Jeremy had always been my cheerleader, repeatedly harping on Dufus: "Dude, when are you gonna get Marie off the market? Seriously though, you *need* to lock that down."

I loved Jeremy for that. He and Rooney seemed to have it figured out; they knew what they wanted in life and saw that in each other and got married. Badda boom, badda bing.

Through my break-up blues, I'd stop at the restaurant Rooney managed to chat and catch up. It was on the way home from the hospital and I wanted to soak up all her feelings about Dufus's extreme stupidity. This was selfish, of course; every woman scorned wants to feel validated. Rooney and I had become somewhat close over the last two years. She always said to me marriage was great but also hard work—things at least I thought I already knew. I'm sure Jeremy, Rooney, Lisa, and Ken were put in a weird spot being thrust awkwardly in-between our break-up (amongst our other mutual friends)—though I told them it wasn't about choosing sides, but sadly we knew things would never be the same.

One night in September, Rooney and I got together outside her workplace, at a taproom in Southeast Portland. The sunny September weather prompted most patrons to lounge at tables outside. Rooney texted me saying she was late, tying things up at work and that she, "Had so much to tell me!"

Oh man, she's pregnant, I thought.

This made me smile. I couldn't wait to tell her about my singleness and show her my List of Dates. I had gotten myself to a place where I wasn't crying every day and was genuinely starting to enjoy myself separate from Dufus. If my heart was a bridge made of matchsticks, I was putting the pieces back together and it was looking like a bridge again.

Rooney arrived. We hugged. She got a beer, sat down, and said, "Jeremy and I are getting divorced."

The matchstick bridge came crashing down.

The traveling Circus of Fun was fractioned ever more. Rooney divulged they were signing papers this week, she had already secured a separate apartment and had moved out, and the divorce was already pretty much done. They were just now starting to tell friends. She seemed sad, but she seemed okay with it, relieved almost.

Well, I wasn't okay with it at all! I didn't get details about the divorce; just that they had been in counseling for quite some time and decided this was the answer. She also divulged that Jeremy and Dufus were going out a lot together, drinking and strip clubs and the like.

On the one hand, I was glad they had each other during a terrible time; on the other hand, I was upset that my beloved cheerleader had probably evaporated, likely cursing women everywhere and the institution of marriage, and on top of all that I was completely overcome with sadness for them, for all of us. It wasn't fair.

We caught up over beers, hugged, and went our separate ways. She had her own journey ahead of her, and I'm sure she wanted to be alone more than I did right then. That night I cried so hard for so long. The brokenness set in again. Hello Square One, nice to see you.

I asked Rooney for permission to message Jeremy, which she of course granted. Like Dufus and I, they didn't want friendships to be split. I wrote Jeremy how utterly heartbroken I was for them, for all of us, and how all I could say was how sorry and how sad I was. We exchanged a few messages of mutual devastation, giving each other encouragement and telling each other it's possible to move on, even though we weren't sure of it ourselves.

Back to rebuilding that bridge, one freaking matchstick at a time.

No. 22
See a classical music performance.

Well, I accidentally crossed this one off after seeing the organ/piano performance at the Old Church. I forgot No. 22 and No. 18 were separate Dates.

No matter, I will allow classic *rock* to substitute.

I freaking love these guys. My all-time favorite road trip music is Crosby, Stills, Nash, and Young's *Four Way Street* album. Their vocal harmony when put to electric guitar makes it impossible for me to sit still. I remember hearing *Suite: Judy Blue Eyes* on the local radio's mix station, turning up the volume in my car, and saying aloud, "Who *is* this?" They more than delivered onstage.

I know what you're thinking. Either: 1.) Who is CSNY? or, 2.) You are WAY too young to know about CSNY.

Choice 2.) is exactly what the older couple said to me as

I sat next to them in the second balcony of the auditorium for the concert. Alright, so what if I didn't go to Woodstock? Who says I can't appreciate antiquated folk rock?

I clapped, I sang, I whistled, I laughed at the crazy antics of David Crosby. I nearly cried when Graham Nash played the piano. And Steven Stills…man, just Steven Stills…yeah, I have no more words.[23]

One of the things Dufus left me was an appreciation for live music I never had before. I guess I do have to admit I have positive takeaways from the relationship, even though it didn't work out the way I wanted it to. It was more than four years of my life, which is at this point only 14%, but I'd be an idiot to believe it didn't change me, for better in some ways. Stephen Stills' voice in the song *Love the One You're With* repeated over and over in my head…

Love the one you're with.

I couldn't think of truer sentiments.

---

23   Neil Young no longer tours with Stills, Nash, and Crosby.

Part 2

The next fifteen Dates

And if some god batters me far out on the wine-blue water,
I will endure it,
keeping a stubborn spirit inside me,
for already I have suffered much
and done much hard work on the waves and in the fighting.
So let this adventure follow.

— Odysseus, Homer's *The Odyssey*, Book 5, 219-224

Sports have always been a big part of my life. My parents believed it paramount to put us kids in team sports to build life skills and constantly strive for excellence, which has translated successfully in adult life…perhaps too much, as I have needed to learn when to "turn off" the competitive switch. This has not been an easy task.

Growing up, I started dance lessons at age four, became competitive at age eight, and didn't stop until eighteen. My family watched college football games fervently, and my siblings and I could sing the Notre Dame fight song by heart upon entering kindergarten. I played soccer from ages five through eleven. There is embarrassing photographic evidence to show preteen years of competitive baton twirling (which I absolutely loved and still geek out over baton twirling videos online). By junior high school I spent weekends performing at football games and dance competitions, and eventually made captain of my high school dance team—some of the best years of my life, to be sure. I was no stranger to rigorous training and discipline. I mean seriously, have you not heard of *Dance Moms*?

By the end of high school, I had had enough. I wanted to be a "normal college student" and opted to not try out for the college dance squad. Instead of filling free time with more rehearsal and practice and endless amounts of hairspray, I wanted to watch movies in dorm rooms. I wanted to play intramural sports without a glance at the scoreboard or a care in the world. I wanted to dominate at beer pong and study hungover in the library. Without any hairspray.[24]

To realize that not everything is a contest was a difficult and painful lesson to grasp, but I managed. By age twenty-seven I've definitely mellowed out…a bit.

No. 41
Try a new sport.

Finding something realistic to attempt proved pretty challenging. I had to rule out flag-football, which I now did year-round on Sundays with an adult intramural coed sports league. "New sport" also nixes any dance-related contests, any soccer, indoor or outdoor. I also had to ignore bowling, kickball, volleyball, basketball, snowboarding, golf (miniature or otherwise), and beer pong (*sigh*). I hate competitive running so triathlons, biathlons, or anything ending with –thlon, was out. If I'm running it has to be to save my ass or catch a touchdown pass. I'm afraid of swinging anything like a bat, so not interested in softball or baseball or hockey. My body was not the gymnastic rubber band it used to be so I didn't want to go too hardcore. I had a physical job and needed to avoid breaking myself for fear

---

24   Thank you, Facebook, for allowing me to chronicle this collegiate reality via kitschy photo albums before I knew that everything on the internet is permanent. I was young, it was 2005. Now I can never run for public office.

of dreaded light duty.

While searching for an option I had flashbacks to freshman year of college when Kumail (celebrity casting: Kumail Nanjiani), an Indian honors student in our coed dorm hallway, tried to teach us how to play cricket. This turned out hilariously disastrous and I decided to go with this vein of thought.

> *Cornhole: also known as Tailgate, bean bag toss and variants, is a lawn game in which players take turns throwing bags of corn at a raised platform with a hole in the far end. A bag in the hold scores 3 points, while one on the platform scores 1 point. Play continues until a team or player reaches the score of 21. –Wikipedia*

September 18th, 2014—I know it is difficult to believe I never played this prior to now. It just wasn't popular where I went to college; Beer Pong and Flip Cup reigned as party activities.

I signed up for a Cornhole league as an individual, as opposed to an already organized team of people. I showed up for the first game held in the garage of a local brew tour company that had recently acquired its beer-serving license. Hello, $4 pints! I met four other individuals, one couple, another single guy and girl, and we named ourselves the Ho Bags. For four weeks, on each Thursday, I met up with them in this garage and tossed bean bags for a few hours while drinking delicious local drafts.

I have to say, as outgoing as I am, I was surprised to find myself remarkably nervous that first night. I was pretty proud of myself for signing up for something I had never done with people I had never met; and guess what, I didn't have to explain my break-up to anyone. Super refreshing.

I missed Week 5 of the league, the playoff day, because I had to work late. The Ho Bags ended up winning the whole thing. While I had a great time over the season, Cornhole wasn't something I wanted to sign up for again, mostly because my work schedule is so variable and it was difficult to get the same night off five weeks in a row, but also because one girl on our team was *kind of over the top.*

The girlfriend half of the couple on team Ho Bags—tall, super slender, celebrity casting Megan Fox—stopped me mid toss once to, "give me some tips on my throw."

Seriously, it's CORNHOLE, lady. It's a drinking game!

I thought about punching her, but I remembered I knew how to turn off my competitive switch now; she obviously did not. I just laughed and accepted the advice graciously, and continued to throw the bean bag wherever I liked. Now, that's successful adulting.

Dancing translated to Drama Club in my youth. Four years of musicals in high school led to college theatre. At age eighteen, pre-adult reality, I did entertain the idea of moving to New York City and trying to really go for it. I thought I was a good enough dancer, even if my singing and acting chops were a real second and third place, but I knew my parents wouldn't pay for a degree in Insecure-Future with a minor in Probable-Low-Income.[25]

---

25   As much as eighteen-year-old me didn't like it, it was the right thing to do, given that no one predicted the market crash of 2008. So, thanks Mom and Dad.

Also, I had a true interest in medicine. I fell in love with nursing as my time in undergrad passed, so I earned a Minor in Theatre while being a total drama groupie. I never landed a main stage casting, but I performed in senior directing projects and smaller shows, not to mention developing a super fun social circle.

After graduating and moving back to Oregon, jobless[26] and socially lifeless, I auditioned and made the cast of a local big (unpaid) musical production. I thought, *Wow it finally happened. Maybe I* don't *need this nursing career after all.* It ran the fall of 2009 and was absolutely grueling. I was back in dance shape and my world again revolved around high kicks, vocal warmups, stretching, icing, Advil, eye makeup, the return of hairspray in my life, and hearing about everyone's next-audition anxiety and need-to-make-rent stress. Performing onstage again had its ultimate highs, as any performer can tell you; but they were small in time compared to the amount of work put in to achieve it. I had to decide whether the benefit was worth the effort, for me, regardless of bills and college debt.

What did I *really* want to do with my life?

Life has a strange way of working itself out. While mentally struggling with whether I should (or even wanted to, or was good enough to) audition again, I landed my first nursing job halfway through the show run. As my professional nursing career took off, I couldn't commit to any sort of rehearsal schedule, so I hung up my dance shoes

---

26   Following the market crash of 2008, the worst unemployment crisis in US history in 70 years wreaked havoc on job-seeking America. Having graduated in the spring of 2009, I—like many millennials and new college grads—endured high debt payments and lower income opportunities, and it took us little while to get our head above water with the rest of America. https://nyti.ms/2kQrqg8

and turned to short story and playwriting—hoping that my immersion in the human condition as a nurse would morph into future creative writing, playwriting, or production. Hey, everyone's got a dream.

Meanwhile, back to journaling the silly antics of being single in my twenties in modern-day Hipster Land…

After deciding not to pursue more performance opportunities after the run of that musical, I promised myself I would audition at least every five years if I wanted to believe myself to be a true theatre artist—even if not performing. "Audition for something" had been on my to-do list for five years. Well, it was now 2014 and my dance shoes were dusty. After a five-year absence from the stage, it was time to remind myself of how completely gut-wrenchingly awful the audition process is.

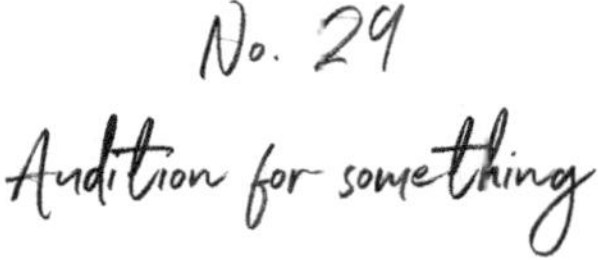

No. 29

Audition for something

A regional theatre company in the area was casting their next season, which included a review of Kander and Ebb. Of all the opportunities in town it was a show that was closest to my wheelhouse, without being in dance shape and karaoke being a poor substitute for vocal practice. I unearthed my vocal study binder from college and pulled out a few Kander and Ebb numbers I had performed in small groups before, think *Cabaret* and *Chicago*.

September 23rd, 2014—I dug out my black character shoes, put on a black pencil skirt, and drove myself out to the theatre complex in rainy traffic at 5:30 p.m. My hands were shaking on the steering wheel as I went through my old vocal warmup. I don't remember the last time I was this nervous; this was way worse than cornhole. I was going to sing on a stage again.

I arrived. I filled out their forms. I attached my old resume and profoundly sad homemade headshot because I wasn't going to front the money for an official one when I wasn't performing or auditioning regularly. I tried not to think about the armpit stains that were forming.

My name was called. I walked in, introduced myself and my songs. I sang "Funny Honey" from *Chicago* and "Who Will Love Me as I Am" from *Sideshow*.

The lovely lady behind the audition table said, "Excellent! Now, you're a full-time registered nurse, it says here?"

I had to explain about the gap in my theatre life as indicated on my resume. I also had to explain why I wrote "probably" under the "List conflicts" section of their audition questionnaire. I had to be honest. With my schedule I couldn't commit to anything but wanted to get out and audition again—even if I wasn't going to make a cast. It was important to me to prove to myself theatre was still a part of my life.[27]

The nice lady behind the casting table said, "Interesting. You're interesting."

Expectedly, I did not hear back from them, which is 100% okay. I went, I sang, I did not pass out, and I left feeling like I could still do the thing. After all, I made my career choice; no one made it for me. I love my job, but maybe someday

---

27   While I keep this tradition of auditioning for something every five years, I don't need it to know theatre is part of my life. I love being an audience member. I go to Ashland, Oregon once a year to experience the Oregon Shakespeare Festival and work on writing. It's an epic trip, and I believe theatre art is important now more than ever. And maybe someday I'll write a play.

I'll work in a doctor's office Monday-Friday 8-5 p.m. and do community theatre again; or maybe I'll continue to love my hospital life and not want to change a thing.

Either way, auditioning was super scary and I wanted it to double count for No. 45. Gigantic self-high-five.

I belted out *Wicked* hits in the car on the way home in rainy traffic, in celebration that *that* was *over*.

No. 23
Attend a McMenamins History Pub

September 29th, 2014—The McMenamins' monopoly is a business empire built on a foundation of brewing craft beer, and has subsequently expanded into the realms of entertainment and hospitality. By practice, the McMenamins brothers take antiquated or falling-apart buildings and turn them into watering holes with popular amusement opportunities. For example, the historic Crystal Ballroom which held early 20th-century dance hall charm and city-wide admiration fell into gross disrepair, housing squatters and likely asbestos from the 1970s through much of the 1990s in downtown Portland. The McMenamins bought it and turned it into a premier staging stop for national music acts, a hotel, four bars, a restaurant, and an underground soaking bath.

I saw the band "fun." play there. Anyway, you get the idea.

A History Pub is a continuing lecture series, one of the many different entertainment type activities one can enjoy at any of the McMenamins locations. On this particular night of history learning/drinking, an author was promoting his new book on the history of climate change at the Kennedy School, a converted elementary school in Northeast Portland (see No. 9).

After waiting an inordinate amount of time to secure libation, I sauntered into the Auditorium full of old couches and cushy chairs, solitary brew in hand. I sat somewhere in the middle, taking in the scene of attendees: a mixture of college students and elderly gray-haired hippie radicals. I figured the author was more toward the latter.

No, he wasn't.

He was young (late-30s I'm guessing), educated, clean-cut, well-spoken and witty, a guest professor at local Reed College, and *FAH-REAK-ING* gorgeous. Celebrity casting Luke Evans.

Professor Evans' presentation of the newly released chronicle on the history and likely dismal future of our planet's climate was not only fascinating, it was very (excuse the pun) down to Earth. He made adorably understandable analogies to describe his research and position. For example, when he used NFL football and beer-drinking in two separate lines of explanation I ABOUT DIED of infatuation. Additionally, the overly cute shout-out to his supportive parents and Grandma in the audience iced the cake.

The Q&A session after the presentation was an entertaining dichotomy of human intelligence and annoying spectacle. Either students stood to ask relevant scientific questions, or the Old Hippies stood up to *not* ask a question but to proselytize a warning of Earthen doom if we humans don't get our shit together and stop raping our planet. Ugh, rude.

"Other *questions* please…" Mr. Evans voiced with emphasis into the microphone, which I viewed as the sexiest underhand way of telling the aging radicals to *shut the fuck up*. My pants were already metaphorically off at this point.

I didn't buy the hardcover at the end of the lecture, and I avoided meeting the illustrious Mr. Evans out of fear I might faint in his presence (the Old Hippies flocked around him for a good thirty minutes following the event anyway) but I did download the book when I got home. I got through the "About the Author" snippet and then internet-stalked him. I found his author bio on Amazon and accompanying headshot. After wiping drool from my chin, I emailed the link to one of my best college friends Maya (celebrity casting: Maya Rudolph), another academic living in Berkeley who would appreciate not only the book but the finer features of the author's lips and jaw line. After hitting *Send* I immediately called Maya and insisted she open the link straightaway, even though she had an infant in one arm and was stirring dinner on the stove with the other hand.

After reading it and seeing his photo, Maya said: "Oh *damn*, girl. This man…this *man*…he is not of this world. He may be out of reach, even for you. I say this with love and concern."

I waited a long time to read his book, out of fear that I might buy a hardcopy and take it to the campus of Reed College to stalk him for a personal signature…or whatever…

No. 32
Go to a Fashion Week event

September 30th 2014—Portland has its own Fashion Week. As an avid *Project Runway* fan, I decided this was the year to go to something. I skipped the bridal couture runway show, for obvious reasons, and got two seats for the Ready to Wear show. Cate was my plus-one. Basically, we were Carrie and Samantha from *Sex in the City*. Other than starting fifty minutes late, the show was everything I'd hoped for—flashy, fabulous, upbeat, and trendy.

I wore my best black pants, my Nine West platform patent leather black heels, and a black-and-white print blouse courtesy of my Buffalo Exchange obsession. I tried to match the ambience as much as possible and think I did a pretty good job—and so did they! It was a super cool show. The runway varied from a coed show, to Thai inspired women's wear, to Northwestern menswear, to a colorful plus-size show, to two young girls' wear shows, and more. Those models do look like a different species, with their weirdly hollow cheekbones and perfectly greased straight legs. All in all, it was a marvelous affair.

To paraphrase Tim Gunn, I really felt like I was making it work.

No. 38

Manicure/Pedicure just because. Not because you have a date or an event or a trip. Just fucking because.

October 3rd, 2014—I spent eight hours enduring a required hospital training session in a warehouse in Northwest Portland. The class incorporated expert instruction from our security staff on self-defense and talk-down interactions for managing aggressive behaviors of patients or visitors gone psycho. This included copious group participation for learning the appropriate physical and verbal manners in which to take down a crazy intoxicated person who is insulted by your substandard care and can't understand why you won't give them more oxycodone.

We had to practice forcing down partners to the matted floor. Additionally, for our viewing pleasure, a wall displayed mounted weapons and sharp contraptions actually confiscated from hospital patients and visitors. Included in this bright whirlwind of optimism were disturbing in-hospital surveillance videos of blunt attacks on staff, an interview with a nurse diagnosed with PTSD after a forceful event, and a wildly uncomfortable finale of a yet-to-be-approved On Campus Shooter protocol—a thing becoming standard practice across the country.[28]

One hour of hand massage and a bold shade of lilac shellac on my fingertips turned my frown right upside-down.

First world problems, am I right?

October 7th, 2014—Here it was, the black and white Oregon Lease Renewal form fresh from my antiquated printer. This past summer I envisioned not having to do this, that I'd be moving out of my spectacular bachelorette pad and shacking up with Dufus to start planning nuptial bliss.

Looking at this form, I knew signing my ever-present maiden name would make me sad no matter how recovered I

---

28   It's really awful that we have to think about this now. Do you work in a hospital? A school? A bank? An airport? A coffee shop? Do you go out in public ever? What is your active shooter plan? Educate yourself: https://bit.ly/1qtOh91

currently felt. It represented an air of finality regarding Dufus's absence from my life, and another year of spouselessness.

To you cursing feminists who now think I'm a total disgrace to independent womanhood, yes I know I don't need to get married to secure contentment. I know. I know I know I know I KNOW I FUCKING KNOW okay BAAAACK OFFFF, put away your lighters and thrift store bras.

My perspective on my own personal pursuit of happiness originates from choosing a career with close proximity to death and suffering. I help sick and dying people for a living. I feel life is much too short and uncertain to do it by yourself. I have held the hand of many people dying alone, without friends or family at all. It is one of the saddest things in the world.

So, my dear loud-and-proud feminists, I do—intensely—value my freedom and independence, but ultimately, I'd like an equal partnership, travel partner/drinking buddy, heterosexual working man who has similar life views as myself, who maybe hates yard work but likes cleaning the kitchen, and wants to rear a few kiddos. I could totally be the yin to that yang. I argue that my choice to look for that self-defined happiness for my own future *is* feminist. However, the yin to my yang can wait, because A.) I haven't detected him on my plane of existence yet, and B.) I have Dates to have with myself first.

No. 42
After renewing your lease, buy something new for the apartment. Something solid.

I signed the 12-month rent lock-in, felt expectedly despondent, and mailed it on the way to IKEA. I wanted to remind myself how fucking badass my solo apartment was and how freaking fabulous the next year was going to be *not* having a roommate/boyfriend to tear my hair out over. Time to rearrange and redecorate.

I know what you're thinking: IKEA and the adjective "solid" aren't exactly synonyms. Originally, I wanted to buy a piece constructed with more sturdiness than particle board. In fact, I was lacking a full-length mirror and longed for something nice, pretty, and well-built. I visited a few shops in the Pearl District and on NW 23rd and soon realized the difference between designer and resale furniture is in the hundreds of dollars region. I was willing to spend up to $200 but couldn't find anything I liked of appropriate size in any of the independent designer stores—see, I tried to stay local. Alas, budgetary reasons brought me to the Swedish Wonderland of home décor and design, which is super fun to go to if you have extra cash, and consequently dangerous to one's wallet.

Did you know at mid-morning on a Tuesday IKEA is filled to the brim with strollers and expectant mothers? I had to navigate my way through a sea of protuberant bellies and screaming toddlers in the IKEA kids' section, which was fine since I didn't need anything there, obviously.

I did pick out a simple full-length mirror with a birch wood frame. I snagged a neat lamp and one or two things for kitchen efficiency. I also found a rolling clothing rack, which is the only thing I had to assemble from hilarious picture directions. I had been trying to find a rack for a while since my closet space at home is brutally limited. The mirror wasn't the elegant design piece I envisioned, but it was simple and reflective, and most of all easy to carry up the stairs by myself. The clothing rack ended up being the most useful and cute addition to my home and with its involvement in No. 44 it was well worth the speeding ticket I earned from the evil photo radar system on the drive home from Swedish Wonderland…must have had rocket fuel in those famous cafeteria meatballs.

No. 44

Sell some clothes at Buffalo Exchange then buy a new article of clothing worth having. Lunch at new place.

I took this idea and turned it inside out. Among the piles of things to get rid of, the clothing heap was the biggest. As I've admitted before, I have an obsession with the recycled fashion store Buffalo Exchange. The staff members are super knowledgeable about current trends and likewise are incredibly stingy when purchasing. It's really tough to bring cash home from that place, but you can opt for store credit and they take extra pieces not purchased and donate to local charity. The downtown location is across the street from Powell's Books and consequently I end up spending hours abusing my credit card between SW 10th and SW 11th Avenues. As much as I love doing this, I had another idea.

The evening of October 7th — After returning home from Swedish Wonderland, I hosted a bunch of ladies in my newly cleaned-out and decorated apartment for a Clothing Exchange. Sometimes called a Naked Lady Party, its purpose is to dig through clothing destined for charity and pick up new outfits for free.

I hung up blankets in my sunroom covering the windows to create a funky changing room. I artfully placed the new mirror there and assembled the clothing rack in my living room. Soon my place was full of clothes, shoes, accessories, and clinking wine glasses.

Many of the gals took home free grabs. To my supreme enjoyment Emma brought a surplus of her fancy stripper shoes. Blake brought this black leather strapless mini dress we all ooh-ed and ahh-ed over. It became the party shtick for every attendee to try it on and model. No, it did not fit everyone; most of us appeared enormously awkward in it, to the amusement of all. Blake's friend Lindsay (celebrity casting: Lindsay Lohan, the only one who did fit in it) ended up taking the black mini dress home.

I took the surplus from the party to Buffalo Exchange on Hawthorne Street later that week. The trendy hipster fashionistas sorted through four large bags of shoes and donated apparel, which garnered about $11.00 in store credit. Some of the items were originally mine so I didn't feel too terrible about using the store credit. I found an awesome part of my Halloween costume (see No. 24). Win.

The items not picked up by the store, which was 80% of the exchange leftovers, were left to the charity of the week: a shelter and a youth theater program. Double win.

I had lunch at a café around the corner. It was not a new place, but I didn't care. They had great cheap breakfast food all day. Dufus and I would go there for brunch sometimes. This memory did not bother me at all as I ate my gooey Eggs Benedict. Triple win.

No. 19
Go to Portland Meadows

October 12th 2014—I can't say I had ever been to a horse race before, but I've been to a casino and I've been to Bi-Mart, and Opening Day at Portland Meadows race track was bizarre offshoot of both.

The week of my 28th birthday had arrived, and I was in the mood to celebrate with friends and behave inappropriately. In recent years, smart creative business people morphed Opening Day at the dilapidated trashy venue into an event other smart creative people wanted to attend. Beer stands, gambling vouchers, drink specials, hot dog carts, photo booths, to name a few of the attractions—but the most auspicious on the day's docket was the Ladies' Hat Competition. Other than the film *My Fair Lady* I have no point of reference as to how hat-wearing became a thing, but it sounded amazing. Also, there was a contest; and I was going to not only knock off No. 21, I was going to win, damnit.

With my history in theatre I take costuming pretty seriously. I spent weeks crafting my straw hat masterpiece in advance. I searched for online pictures of winners past, many presenting with horse themes. Somehow my brain arrived at that moment in *The Wizard of Oz* where Dorothy and company climb onto a horse-drawn carriage led by an iridescent purple horse inside Emerald City, and the gentleman driving the coach refers to their colorful leader as a horse of a different color.[29] Then the group takes off singing. The horse changes from purple to orange and then to yellow. I ran with this theme of unique individuality, wanting to highlight my own personal quirkiness in the hat design. I went to junk stores and fabric outlets and picked out a few neat items. I hauled out my craft supply bins, hot glue gun, and came up with the masterpiece. It was a broad straw hat with little mold to it. Carefully with straight pins, I attached signage with the phrase *Now That's a Horse of a Different Color!* to the brim in black glittery lettering against a gold glittery background. I wrapped a gold scarf around the hat for the band, allowing it to fall attractively off the back. I attached several small charming junk pieces to the scarf and pinned three large silk flowers to the back. On the front I secured a miniature version of the movie scene, a print on cardstock of Dorothy and company looking at the purple Horse of a Different Color.[30]

It was sparkly, nifty, and had just enough spunk. I wore

---

29   According to the American Heritage® Idioms Dictionary, the phrase originates from Shakespeare's *Twelfth Night* Act 2, Scene 3 "a horse of that color" which meant "the same manner" rather than a difference. By the mid-19th century the phrase colloquially meant the opposite in common English, to point out the blatantly dissimilar.

30   To see photos of the hat (and other things from the List experiences) head to my website mariemacmillan.com/rebootphotos

it proudly into the entrance of Portland Meadows. Blake took my picture in front of the Goorin Brothers' table, the local hat shop sponsoring the contest. This was to be posted on Instagram for the social media masses to see and like. My understanding was this online posting *was* the entry and a winner would be announced in a week. I was sure I had the cat in the bag and walked off in my dress and high heels with my crew for the day: Blake, her boyfriend Jake, his nice-but-awkward friend Daniel (Daniel Radcliffe), and my definitely-just-platonic guy friend Adam (Adam Brody) and his friend Chris (Chris Pine).

With cans of free beers in our hands, we watched the whole procedure take place: the warming up of horses, the inspections inside the stalls, and the parading out to the starting gate. The actual races were short. Everyone stopped what they were doing to watch them lap around the track, and cheer and hoot and holler when they wound around to the finish.

And in such spectacular, moderately drunken fashion, I enjoyed myself so much I didn't hear the overhead announcement and call for Hat Judging at 3 p.m. The contest came and went without my crowning. The realization came with shock and sadness, and a slow motion closeup of my face mouthing the word, "No!!!"

Apparently, I wasn't going to knock off No. 21 after all, but I didn't let it bother me for too long. We spent several hours reveling in the extravaganza. I didn't stay until the bitter end of the racing, mostly because I'd had enough beer and wanted something to eat besides a hot dog Blake and I made our way to Southeast Portland and stopped for barbecue. It was delicious. So delicious. I mean, it was

"I'm-drunk-and-hungry" delicious, but the whole day was delicious. Several people commented on my hat and entire outfit (*Girl, I love your outfit, you are put together!*) and Dan awkwardly flirted with me. I enjoyed stares from both sexes as I towered at six feet in a pair of Emma's famed platforms pawned from the Clothing Exchange. If I caught myself in a reflective surface I thought, *oh hell yes.*

Chewing on my spicy barbecue sandwich, gulping down water, I reflected on the day's ultimate self-confidence boost. I was having an epiphany. I looked hot and felt hot for the first time in a long time, and relished the fact that others took notice. Trying to remember what a man's appreciation felt like, I forgot how tipsy I was and let Blake talk me into downloading a popular dating app called Tinder.

Blake was on it. Jake was on it. Adam was on it. Dan and Chris didn't admit or deny its usage. I decided that short term romantic entertainment was in order. I mean, I was that much closer to the big 30 now, time to test the waters.

Those of you who have Tinder-ed before can only imagine the hijinks that ensued. I knew there would be hijinks, but I didn't think they would become anecdotal legend.

I thought wrong.

Side Story #4
The Tinder Distractions

Oh man.

Oh man, oh man, oh man.

I say that because that's exactly what this convoluted cyber distraction amounted to. For those of you unfamiliar with Tinder, I'll provide a brief description.

Tinder is a smartphone dating app which takes three pieces of information: preferred age range, preferred gender(s), and preferred radius of miles to find available individuals. The app takes the selected criteria and displays other Tinder users meeting these discovery settings. Potential matches are displayed only one at a time, and the thing about Tinder that separates it from other more cumbersome dating sites that it is almost solely powered by physical appearance. After settings are programmed in, *bam!* Behold, a headshot of a 31-year-old male with a solitary sentence describing himself, "Hi I'm Brad, I'm new in town and looking for new friends and fun!" Simple and effective.[31] Hey, they do say first impressions are everything.

You can display just your name and age, or rant on for a paragraph that no one will read. Like accessorizing, less is more. Now here is the addicting part: after looking at Brad's 1-6 photos and optional description you decide to *Swipe Right* to "Like" him—or *Swipe Left* to dislike or "Nope" him. It's similar to the predecessor web game *Hot or Not*. If two users both *Swipe Right* or "Like" each other, then a cute little *It's a Match!* screen pops up and you have the ability to message within the application.

Here's the catch: Tinder has a reputation for being a hookup venue, a lions' den of lechers just waiting for consenting partners. Without having any experience with it myself, I proclaimed to Blake that it lies on the spectrum of online dating somewhere above Craigslist personal ads but

---

31   Like many dating apps, I believe Tinder has evolved over the years, but this is how it worked in 2014. Also, there was never a real Brad, it's just an example name. Not satisfied, Brads of Portland area? Okay fine, let's go with celebrity casting Brad Pitt.

below free OkCupid; and, with said reputation comes the inevitable solicitation for casual encounters, as described by Blake and Emma and other male and female friends alike.

I was hesitant to even sign up for it because of the bad date stories, but my birthday shenanigans had me thinking it would be something fun to try out. I hadn't been on a date in months (let alone get laid) and was thinking short-term male entertainment was just what the doctor ordered.

"Get back on the horse, Marie," Adam said.

"Just try it. It's fun," Blake said.

Fine, giddy-up.

You know what, I totally and completely forgot there are levels of dating between we're-just-friends and this-is-my-serious-boyfriend/almost fiancé. Really, I forgot that casual dating was a thing I used to do, and that it can be fun and not stressful. In truth, I was surprised about Tinder—it was FUN. Not only was it like a game where you get to be the ultimate judge of other people's faces, it was a fascinating sociological experiment. I was thankful not to fill out loads of questionnaires or be required to read lengthy profiles. To my delight, I found many attractive male users between the ages of 30 and 35 within a 20-mile radius of me also seeking light-hearted short-term romantic endeavors.

It proved awfully effective. Within fourteen hours of having the damn thing on my phone I had plenty of matches, and I already set up a date.

Distraction #1

I was having a panic attack in the car on the way to this obscure bar where I'd meet Joel (celebrity casting choice: Joel McHale, host of *The Daily Soup*). I parked and began practicing deep breathing while clutching my steering wheel for dear life. I hadn't been on a first date in over two years and hadn't been on any kind of date with a boy in months.

It's just a beer, I repeated to myself. *You can leave whenever you want to. You can do this. It's no big deal. Just get out of the car.*

I opened my car door and got out. I walked into the obscure meeting place and found the guy sitting at the bar looking around just as nervously as I was. We shook hands, said hello; I ordered a beer, and supreme awkwardness followed. He looked older and less good-looking than his pictures (Welcome to online dating, right? No disrespect, real Joel McHale). We proceeded to the regular, "So, what do you do? Where are you from?" pleasantries which eventually led to Joel recounting the last time he was in this specific bar, and how he got kicked out.

Nice. I raised my eyebrows in as neutral expression as I could muster.

"Well, that was back in my wild days. I had a hard life until the last few years," he explained.

"Oh, so when did you get out of the slammer?" I chuckled, taking a swig of beer.

"Well…" he trailed off.

Shit. Oops.

"I was young when it happened," Joel added, creepily stroking a piece of hair around my ear.

Whaaaaat noooo eeggghhhh…

Stroke is too nice a word for what happened. Really, what he did was pet a plait of hair, not with his fingers but with the palm of his hand, like one would pet a horse. His sweaty fingers dragged slowly down my cheek and neck. My eyeballs popped out of my head. The word creepy just does not cut it. I leaned away from the obviously failed gesture with wide-eyed finesse. I thought it would end there, but no.

I turned my torso away from him and squared my shoulders with the bar. Joel then bent his head sideways so his left temple rested on my right shoulder for a brief moment, like a cat trying to rub its ears on a scratch post. I'm not sure, but I think a purring noise came out of him.

I made no noise. My mouth opened silently, in a gasp of horror.

Okay, date over. I moved to gather my purse.

After about sixty total minutes I was able to pay and get up from the cursed barstool and walk to the exit. Joel followed behind, almost apologetically. I think he was surprised I was not into his, um, *style*. It was very clear, to both of us, that there was no chemistry. He was obviously not short-term entertainment material, and I was not a cat.

However, we hugged politely (*ick*) and he said, "It was very nice meeting you."

"Likewise," I replied. Classy to admit defeat, I have to say.

After shaking off the weird cat vibe on the way to my car, I drove home with newfound confidence. Despite Tinder Fail #1, I went on a date and the sky didn't come crashing down, and I didn't go running back to Dufus. I thought, *Hey that wasn't so bad. I could do that again*—minus the weird petting.

Distraction #2

My second first date in recent memory came just a few days later. Different bar. Different part of town. Different guy. Much younger, in fact I bent my age-range a bit. I altered the parameters on my account after Distraction #1 to include men ages 28-35. Note: I was excluding men older than 35 to avoid seeing a likely-existing profile of 39-year-old newly-single Dufus.

Distraction #2, aka Justin (celebrity casting choice: 1998 Justin Timberlake) turned twenty-eight just a few months before me.

We met at a downtown dive bar. Immediately, I could tell he was way easier to talk to and way easier on the eyes. He kind of had this whole '90s Justin Timberlake thing down, the blonde curls, the sporty clothing, the sweet charm—you can imagine it had an effect on a girl who was once twelve-years-old and *NSYNC obsessed. We talked about sports and the city, what we liked and didn't like, he bought me a drink, I bought him a drink; we learned we shared several interests.

After a few hours he walked me to my car, and kissed me.

I pulled away from him surprised for a minute thinking, *Wait, hang on, do I remember how to do this? …Those blonde curls…Oh yeah, I do.*

We made out a bit, exchanged phone numbers, and said adieu until next time.

Next time? Hold the phone; was this leading to a second date? No worries. *Breathe.* Casual, casual, casual. Be cool… everything is fine.

The second date was a few days later. He asked if I wanted to see a movie, I said sure. He picked me up, we saw the movie. He was trying hard to be boyfriend-esque during the film, holding my hand, wrapping his arm around my shoulder, etc. For some reason I thought it was cute, and I fantasized for a moment a time machine had spit out actual 1998 Justin Timberlake onto 2014 Tinder. He drove me home and we made out in his car.

Hey Mom and Dad, do yourself a favor and skip to Distraction #3 now. The details in the upcoming paragraphs are not super important for you. Summary: It didn't work out. Readers, stop reading aloud to conservative Grandma, unless she's cool.

"So, do you want to get a beer at the Corner Bar?" he asked.

"You know the beer is free upstairs in my apartment," was my reply, loaded with intentional innuendo.

It finally clicked.

Good ol' skilled-at-casual-dating Marie reappeared with cool indifference and invited a gentleman caller upstairs with the sole purpose of having informal premeditated sex. Finally. Because it had been months. And I really wanted to. And because I'm a woman of the 21st century and I can do what, sorry who, I want. We were gonna bang, damnit.

He grinned and agreed whole-heartedly. (Duh.) At lightspeed, we made it to my couch where clothes and shame were shed without a second thought.

And…it…wasn't…great.

I didn't expect amazing the first time around, even for my prepubescent major crush, but something was off. Either he couldn't find a rhythm, or I was doing something wrong. I mean it had been a few months for me sure, but not long enough to forget where things go. He just…didn't seem to be enjoying himself. He was staring at my TV, which was turned off. He was mentally elsewhere, distant and uninterested.

"Are you okay? Am I doing something wrong?" I finally asked.

"No, no, just give me a minute," Justin remarked, doing the exact same thing.

"Okay," I replied withstanding the awkward repetitive action.

A minute later I said, "Are you sure? You seem…I mean we can move—"

He stopped moving.

"I dunno, I just…" he panted out, and with sincere desperation he looked up at me and said, "This is just happening so fast."

What. The fuck.

The dude was literally inside me while saying it. I sat there, on top of him, stunned. Utterly stunned. I was sexually infuriated. Five minutes ago, while he was tearing open the condom wrapper from his jacket pocket, would have been a better time to admit that. Or seven minutes ago when I was helping him undo his belt. Or even ten minutes ago when we walked up my stairs. Or fifteen minutes ago in his car when I invited him upstairs. Seriously, *what the fuck!!!* I certainly don't remember drugging and dragging him up to my couch. He entered my apartment (and the double entendre) willingly, soberly, and prophylactically prepared, so *I know* he knew what was up.

Dear every guy I physically teased between the years of 2005 and 2007, I get you now; I'm so sorry. I wanted to yell all these things at him, but instead I shut my eyes, pursed my lips, ignored my girl case of blue balls and uttered, "Okay. I'm gonna get up now."[32]

I put on clothes, cracked open two beers from my fridge and plopped myself back on the couch while he headed to

____

32   It's really funny and interesting to read this after the birth of the #metoo movement. I've had my own thoughts about sexual consent and my own history, so I'm glad to know that as soon as 1998 Justin Timberlake expressed discomfort with the situation I stopped. Way to not be rapey, Marie.

my bathroom, probably to finish himself off. Great. Just fucking great.

What did I do wrong?

"Hey what did I do wrong?" I asked when he reemerged to put on pants. I offered him the second beer. "If you don't want it I'll drink it."

Justin took the beer. "You didn't do anything wrong. You're very hot," he explained conciliatorily. I felt marginally better, and then something occurred to me.

"Is this…not something…you do?" I asked.

Oh shit. He's a virgin. I just took his V-card.

"No, no, I do this. I knew what was up," he replied. I was halfway reassured. "I don't know what is wrong with me, I think, I don't know…"

He went on to elaborate on how he didn't know what he wanted from women or commitment, blah blah blah, stuff I didn't care about. Good Lord. I tried to simplify things for him by explaining my mission, Captain Kirk style: to seek out new life and new fornication.

He wanted to try sex again, but I shot him down: "Sorry, sweetheart, that was a one-time special." I wasn't getting on that merry-go-round again just to get thrown off.

Justin nodded and gathered his things. I felt bad for him, not 100% convinced he wasn't a virgin half an hour prior. I think he tried—really, something just stopped him for whatever reason. I like to think the reason had nothing to do with me, but Jesus, could he have had that moment of epiphany *before* we ripped our clothes off?

Feeling defeated, I walked him to my door and told him, "Hey, you know beside the weirdness, it was a really nice night."

"Believe me, it wasn't you," Justin said giving me a hug.

"I know," I replied, patting him on the shoulder.

I shut and locked my door, palm to forehead. I turned around and saw that my stupid, low quality IKEA couch was not in its original sitting place. Like at all. Since a few textbooks were the only things holding up the right rear corner, our unsuccessful gyrations had shifted the cursed thing halfway across the living room, diagonally askew—like my attempt at short term romantic encounters. I shoved it back in place and stuffed the old textbooks back under the legless corner. I immediately called the only other person I thought would be awake and willing to hear my Tinder drama at 11:45 p.m.

[*Dial tone*] "Hello?"

"Adam, you will not believe what just happened. Some guy blue balled me, big time."

"Like how bad?"

[Insert vivid retelling of sexcapade failure.]

"Oh, that's fucked up. I'm sorry. It's not you."

"I guess. I don't know, Adam, this Tinder thing isn't really cutting it. Maybe I'm not good at it," I replied.

"Not possible," Adam encouraged me, "You are a single girl looking for unattached fun. There are literally hundreds of dudes who will take you up on that."

"Yeah, but how many of them are douche bags, gross, or creepy?" I asked.

"Most."

"Ah screw it, I'm done with this stupid thing."

"Nooooo! Don't give up!" Adam pleaded, "I just got done with a mediocre Tinder date tonight, and I'm back to swiping!"

"Ugggggghhhhh," I replied with wordless frustration noises.

"Stay on the horse woman!"

Distraction #3

I noticed several repeating themes in my waterfall of eligible cyber bachelors. I feel the need to list my observations from this bizarre social experiment, notably:

- ❖ Put it right next to your TripAdvisor app.
  - o "Hey I'm in town for the weekend, anyone wanna show me around?" Apparently, because Tinder uses GPS location, it is a popular method of finding a local "tour guide" with optional undergarments. Made me wonder just how single those guys are in their hometowns.
- ❖ Please no hookups.
  - o Adam tells me this is a phrase that frequents the female profiles on Tinder. Since I'm unable to see the women (because I haven't checked female as a gender I'm interested in) I'll take his word for it. However, I have run across a few men touting their attempts at "finding The One." I wanted to tell them I don't think this is their ideal situation in which to meet spousal material, though I'm sure Tinder is not the only form of virtual romance they're involved in.
- ❖ Hookups only.
  - o Conversely, the Nothing Serious attitude was more prevalent among the male population of Tinderland. I saluted the refreshingly stark honesty by Swiping Right on only one or two of these seemingly creditable

gents. I received one lustful, "DTF?"[33] message which I did not reply to, and one conversation that went like this:

> <Nothing Serious:> Hey can I tell you a secret?
>
> <Me:> I don't know, can you?
>
> <Nothing Serious:> I'm super hung.
>
> No reply. Unmatch. Even if this is true, no worthy guy comes out to say it.

- ❖ Seeking friendship.
    - o "Hi, I'm married, but I'm just on Tinder to find friends and companionship." Translation: I don't want my wife to see this. We have problems.
- ❖ Seeking playmate.
    - o "Hi, this is me and my amazing wife/girlfriend. We'd like to find a fun-loving friend to complete our circle on occasion." Translation: We have no boundaries and like sex sex sex sex sex sex sex. We have problems.
- ❖ Seeking everything.
    - o I had to Google "pansexuality."

In addition to the above phenomena, I found certain repetitive traits that had me automatically *Swiping Left* (or "Nope"). Recently, I was inspired by a spectacular book entitled *Adulting: How to Become a Grownup in 468 Easy(ish) Steps* (see Appendix A). Full of brilliant graphs and penned doodles, author Kelly Williams Brown really hits her points home with ingenious finesse. I took a leaf from Kelly Williams Brown and illustrated my thought process in algorithm

---

33   In romantic text message shorthand, "Down to fuck?" You know, *real* classy twenty-first century pickup line.

form. I sketched this gem on scrap paper and showed it to a select few people who can corroborate, factually, that I had this masterpiece tacked on my fridge *before* the next date with Bachelor No. 3 (See Figure 1. Marie's Unfortunate Tinder Algorithm).

All of the boxes in the algorithm came from actual Left Swipes, except for two. I never saw a cat with a lip piercing, and aside from this next one the remainder of the boxes truthfully were inspired by immediate rejections.

Please notice the top of Figure 1 where the famous SNL sketch "Dick in a Box" is mentioned. If by some social media miracle you have not seen this, watch it now.[34] While irreverently hilarious, real Justin Timberlake and real Andy Samberg can pull this shit off. Hello, it's *Saturday Night Live*.

Dear real dudes at large: having this as your Tinder profile picture IS NOT attractive to me. Do you really think you're going to get laid by touting women with the idea that your penis is so mind-blowing it is a gift to humanity? I mean, I guess it's funny among friends, but not to people you don't know but might be romantically or sexually interested in…gross.

Tinder Distraction No. 3. Ashton (celebrity casting: Ashton Kutcher) passed the increasingly stringent Swipe test. He was also a staunch Timbers fan and we clicked on many levels in our messaging prior to meeting. We met at a neutral site mere days after 1998 Justin Timberlake walked out of my apartment (aka, Tinder Fail #2).

I arrived first. Ashton walked in while I was sipping on my first beer.

Hi, how are you? —polite hug—*So nice to meet you.*

---

34 SNL Digital Short "Dick in a Box," 2006 https://bit.ly/2UOmlSR

I was speaking Blind Date fluently by now.

Ashton—works in finance, well-dressed—spoke about how today was his first $100 haircut and how his next big purchase was going to be a boat for his Lake Oswego[35] residence. Halfway through his monologue on real estate investment being the best thing ever, I presumptuously categorized Ashton as generically good-natured money-monger from the West Side while I was sure he was labeling me as sassy sarcastic blue-collar chick from the East Side. The differences were apparent, but let's not get too *West Side Story* here. We were both employed single adults with similar sports and pop culture interests, which took us to a different venue for drink number two.

As we looked for the next choice of watering hole, the subject of conversation turned to Halloween. I explained my plans to attend a concert downtown. Ashton then got super excited and divulged his oh-so-original plan.

Ashton leaned forward, smiling conciliatorily, "Oh, me and my buddy have the BEST costume ever!"

"Oh yeah?" I replied.

"Oh yeah, it's hilarious. We are going to kill it! It's sooooo good."

"Wow. What is it?"

"So you remember SNL's Dick in a Box right?"

Insert uncontrollable laughter on my part. Behold, Tinder Fail #3. If he only knew, he had just been Swiped Left. Nope to you! What a revelation. Seriously, I'm not making this up. This really happened.

---

35   A wealthy city/suburb within the Portland metroplex

Figure 1. Marie's Unfortunate Tinder Algorithm

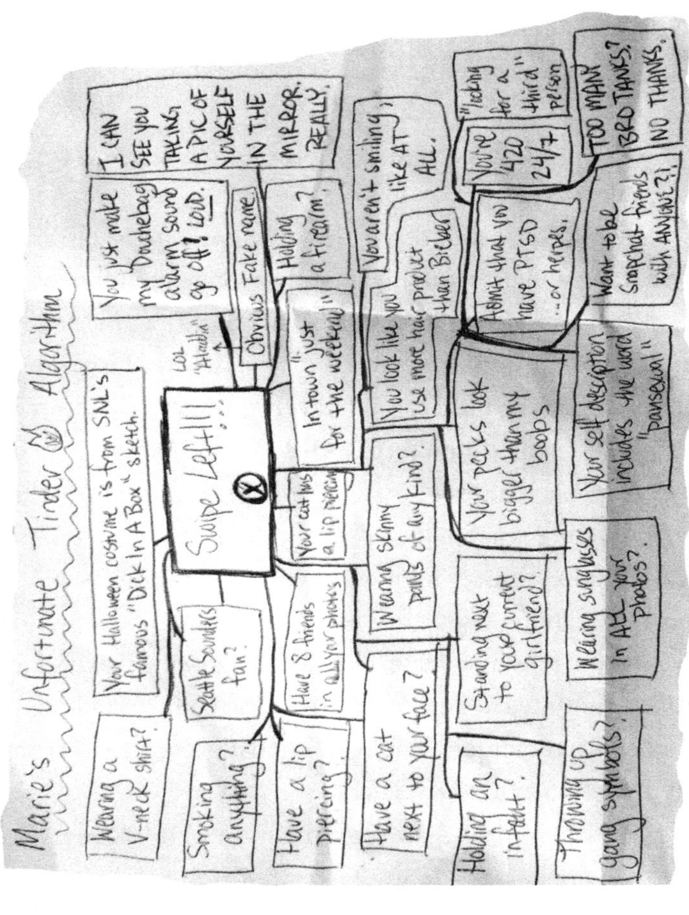

The date wasn't all bad, I just thought it was hilarious that he self-identified with one of the premeditated boxes on my Unfortunate Tinder Algorithm tacked to my refrigerator at home. I mean the guy unknowingly Swipe-Left-ed himself.

Ashton and I ended up Facebook friending each other, in the event we'd need ticket exchanges once soccer season returned. Again, nice guy, but no sparks—for either of us.

"It was nice meeting you," he said at the end of the date.

Well, it was nice meeting you too, Tinder. It was great fun, I've got to say.

Twelve days, four dates, three different guys, one failed sexual encounter, and many data alerts on my cellphone plan.

What a social workout. I felt like I completed a bachelorette triathlon. I'd like to say I never had any awkward sightings of them ever again, but I can't. I never came across Tinder Fail #1, Joel McHale, again but Tinder Fail #3, Ashton Kutcher, and I saw each other at various Timbers games throughout the following season. It was only slightly awkward. Tinder Fail #2 unexpectedly showed up in preparation for No. 16.

I put Tinder away after that.[36] I still played the Swiping game every now and again, but I was dismissing it as a serious option for practical match-making. The Unfortunate Tinder Algorithm remained visible on my fridge as a testament to my Finally Getting Out There.

I was proud of the accomplishment; however, I was ready to get back to dating Yours Truly.

Exclusively.

---

36   False. I did not put Tinder away. See Side Story #7.

No. 48

Go to an event that requires singing. (In the shower does not count.)

I noticed a new sign apparent on the sidewalk outside The Corner Bar, advertising karaoke night:

> *Trust me, you can sing. –Vodka*

October 17th, 2014…I think? This date seems wrong, but oh well it's what is written down on the List…While this was not my first time singing publicly (see No. 29) I took the sign as a sign. I rocked my Tinder woes away to Wheatus' *Teenage Dirtbag* and got on a first-name basis with the KJ, who wrote me a facetious scribbled note on a napkin and left it on top of my beer: "This drink has roofies in it."

It didn't. How do I know? I drank the beer anyway. Because, alcohol.

Only five people were there for Karaoke. We weeknight patrons few had a five-person song rotation that included the bartender. I performed a duet with a complete stranger. It became a night to reminisce about every time I see those four other special people.

Alright, I have a bar problem—no, not an alcohol problem, a *bar* problem—given the KJ, door dude, and several bartenders Facebook-friended me, and because that napkin note is still on my fridge next to Marie's Unfortunate Tinder Algorithm, *and*—more notably—because I adore all of these things and am not ashamed to tell people so.

No. 33
Attend a festival you haven't been to

October 18th, 2014—Originally, for No. 33 I was envisioning something ridiculous, like a professional fire jugglers' festival or something very Portland level of weird. I had been to several of the area beer festivals, but wanted something a little more off kilter for my List. Shockingly, I couldn't find anything along these lines in the next few weeks, but it was near enough to Halloween that several pumpkin-related festivities were happening in and around town. I was confidant I'd find something.

Sometime between Tinder Fail #2 and Tinder Fail #3, I decided to distract myself in other less disappointing ways. For October, it was absolutely gorgeous outside, warm enough to wear shorts, and the itch to get out of town was scratching. I took only my purse and a water bottle and drove eastward on I-84.

I got up and went as soon as the idea struck. I didn't have to check in with anyone or ask for permission. I marveled at how lucky I was to be able to do such things. I drove past Multnomah Falls and went on to exit at Hood River, just under an hour drive. I parked downtown up on a hill and walked down to the banks of the mighty Columbia River where the Hood River Harvest Festival was in full swing. I paid for three hours of parking and told myself to spend all of that time absorbing the autumnal celebration.

How to describe the scene at hand, hmm…a farmer's market on crack? It was larger, more expansive, with even more euphoria. It felt different from the farmers' markets in the city because those farmers haul their produce from farther away. The plethora of harvest crops in front of me didn't have to travel far. Pallets upon pallets of pears, beets, potatoes, enough apples to build a three-bedroom house with indoor plumbing and cable television lined the market avenues. Rows of fresh flowers and greenery surrounded me. Grandiose tents holding fifty plus vendors stood next to a beer garden overlooking the banks of the river. Festival goers ranged from small children, family groups, teenage clicks, grown-up beer/wine/cheese/art connoisseurs, and solo adventurers alike—all of us equally elated to find not a solitary cloud in the sky.

I took my time walking amidst it all. I stopped to watch a pie-eating contest sponsored by Pacific Gas & Electric, whose big-headed mascot was a crowd favorite. I marveled at the largest pumpkin in the county, and the man carving different faces into it. I visited every wine and beer vendor to try out what they had to offer. I spent time talking to jewelry artists, soap makers, scarf knitters, quilters, painters, and photographers. I bought Christmas presents for family and friends. I had quite the pile of goodies going. I took my harvest yield and sauntered to the river's edge where many were lying in the warm October sun, soaking in the last of it before it vanished until March or April or May.

I spent the end of my three hours lying on the grassy hill, resisting the urge to join a few kids rolling down like logs. I laughed with them as they ran back up the hill and did it over and over and over again.

The booze samples must have gotten to me, or the sun, or the inimitable human feeling of…genuine happiness.

I am by myself and I am content.

Even if it was fleeting, I realized I had left whatever residual sorrow I held onto at home. I purposefully removed myself from it successfully, for an entire day.

I celebrated the newish sentiment by treating myself to dinner at a renowned local restaurant and took a leisurely drive home, following the sun westward as it dipped behind the coastal mountain range. I was gone for only part of the day, so this little trip couldn't count for No. 46, but it sure felt like I had been somewhere over the rainbow.

No. 24
See something at Roseland Theater

As you may have gathered, some of my Dates took research and planning. In addition to the Crosby, Stills, and Nash concert, I also saw Foster the People at McMenamin's Edgefield with my brother Andy. Despite my newfound interest in live music, I hadn't been to the Roseland Theater downtown—a smaller venue that once had Prince grace its stage. While browsing upcoming shows at the historic theater, I clicked on each upcoming artist to test out their music styles, including newer rap artists trying to make a fresh break into the industry, or DJ shows. I like rap, and I like house music, but none of the upcoming acts resonated with me until I came to the group listed for October 31st: a lesser known musical act called St. Lucia.[37] I learned that South African lead singer Jean-Philip Grobler remixed tracks for other known bands like Passion Pit and Foster the People. St. Lucia's indie-electronic, synthpop funky beats had me

---

37   http://stlucianewyork.com/

totally mesmerized.

I first downloaded their album *When the Night* while researching for Dates back in August—and the song *September* had me feeling hopeful as I burned that piece of paper in my sunroom described in Side Story #1, right before the smoke alarm drowned out the bass beats. After months of listening to the album, I bought four tickets to the Halloween concert at $18.00 each. I knew, I just knew, this was going to be an epic experience.

The end of October came around and my friends were exchanging ideas for Halloween plans. What bars would be cool? Who didn't have kids and had the evening free to act like one? Newly-divorced Jeremy was still going to throw the annual Halloween bash at his house, even though Rooney had moved out. Lisa called me asking if I was going to come or not. I told her and Ken to have a good time without me. Part of the reason the Halloween concert was so appealing to me was that I could have the excuse of big epic plans and that way I didn't have to feel bad about not making an appearance at Jeremy's party, where I knew Dufus would be—a party where we competed for best couple's costume the last two years, getting second place to Jeremy and Rooney twice, talking trash all year about how we were definitely going to win this time.

So, due to sour grapes as described above, I wasn't exactly excited about Halloween festivities. However, having the concert to look forward to made it bearable; that, and I grew more infatuated with the band. I had *When the Night* on continuous repeat.

The week of the concert I gave Blake and her boyfriend Jake two of the tickets. I had high hopes of finding a date, thinking Jake's awkward friend Daniel Radcliffe from my racetrack birthday shenanigans might do, but he was non-committal when I asked—and if anything was unattractive to me now it was a man afraid or hesitant to make a decision.

My buddy Adam already had tickets to another bigger concert at the Rose Garden arena. He told me to put "need a date for Halloween" on my Tinder profile.

Haha, no. I thought.

On October 30th I was running out of options, but I thought I'd have more self-respect than troll for a blind date on Tinder. I didn't want to sell the remaining ticket, but it was looking like I'd have to. Oh well, I wouldn't mind going stag; I could make friends. Plus, it was the show I was most anticipating.

Hello, Mr. Craig List, would you like to do the work for me?

Within a few hours of posting the ticket I had inquiries. I told the first offer to meet me at The Corner Bar to pick up the ticket for face value. I'm not sure what I was expecting, but a tall, blonde, cute, twenty-three-year-old Southern guy who just moved to the area two weeks ago and knew nobody *was not* it. Celebrity casting choice: Josh Hutcherson, from *The Hunger Games.*

Seriously, all I had to do was post a concert ticket on Craigslist and the internet would spit out a non-creepy cute single guy? If I'd known it was that easy earlier…I take back my comment about Craigslist being below Tinder in the taxonomy of online dating. Josh sat down with me at the bar after paying for the ticket, and we chatted a bit before he had to leave.

"Hey, I'd stay for a beer but I have to work tomorrow,

sorry," Josh said, looking genuinely hesitant to leave.

"No worries. Hey if you want to hang out during the concert, just let me know. I know you said you don't know many people here, no pressure though," I added, legitimately trying to be nice to a person new to the city.

"Oh, I thought you were selling the ticket because you couldn't go."

"Oh, no I'm going! I just didn't have a plus-one. It's totally okay if you don't want to, no big deal, I was just trying to get rid of the ticket."

"No, sounds good. I'll see you there!" Josh said, and we exchanged phone numbers because we had been using the Craigslist email forward to communicate; off he went into the rain and traffic. I sat there with my beer, contemplating the serendipity.

October 31st, 2014—I had my costume all ready to go. Just because I wasn't competing in a couple's contest didn't mean I wasn't going to dress up. Come on, I don't say no to a costume party (except the one I was avoiding by going to a concert). I put effort into collecting a pretty rad ensemble. Deciding to carry on my *Wizard of Oz* theme from the Portland Meadows horse races, I morphed into Grunge Dorothy for concert night.

I met at Blake's apartment to get ready. She was putting zombie makeup on Jake and getting her outfit together. Awkward Dan (Daniel Radcliffe) was there, flirty as ever.

Apparently, he thought *he* was going to the concert with us.

"What?! Um, no I sold the ticket last night!" I exclaimed. "You never got back to me about it," I crossed my arms, utterly frustrated. Dan was a nice guy, just clearly didn't know what he wanted in this universe. We finished our costumes, downed some cans of PBR, and hit the road, leaving Awkward Dan to walk back to his apartment. I felt bad, but it was fleeting. He didn't bring a costume. You have been judged.

Strutting down Burnside Street on Halloween night was quite a sight to behold. I mean, the occupants of downtown Portland don't usually make my head turn with all the weirdos dressed up on a normal basis (again, the Unipiper), but tonight was especially radical. Turns out, most of the concert-goers dressed up, too. I patted myself on the back, thinking my homemade red-glitter tennis shoes, black hair weave, temporary arm sleeve tattoo, and an impulse-purchase studded denim vest were 100% worth the effort.

I spotted my Craigslist mystery guy Josh pretty soon after entering the Roseland Theater. He skipped the costume and went with a classy polo and jeans look. I introduced him to Blake and Jake, aka Grunge Wicked Witch and Zombie Soccer Player. Josh and I bantered on and on about how off-our-rockers crazy we were for this band. The opening act was supposed to be amazing too, a young DJ by the name of Robert DeLong. Okay, minor tangent: bear with me here. So, I may have hinted at this before—but I'm kind of a nerd. Fellow nerds may have picked up on this, but if not, here's the official confession: I am a sci-fi watching, Star-Trek quoting, Firefly-DVD-owning, Han-Solo-T-shirt-wearing Nerd with a capital N. I didn't ever get into comic books, video games, cosplay, RPG, conventions, or renaissance fairs so I'm not entirely sure that puts me into Geek territory—one could extrapolate further where exactly I lie on the spectrum of nerdiness, but let's not waste time. Back to the concert, and the absolute nerdgasm[38] that the first act gave me.

Robert DeLong's setup crew came out wearing jeans and uniform tops from *Star Trek: The Next Generation*. Then Robert DeLong came out in that powder blue science officer uniform singular to babe-alicious Dr. Beverly Crusher. Then, he Crushed it, with a capital C. The dude showed serious talent, recording and replaying his own voice into the thumping tracks—'90s-fashion square TV screens showing psychedelic sci-fi screenshots behind him. Josh and I nodded our heads to the bass beat, sipping on beers. Blake and Jake were grooving as well. I thought the nerdgasm would end with the first act, but no. Headlining St. Lucia brought the house down, *a galaxy far far away* style.

Lead singer Jean-Philip Grobler came out onstage with his guitar, in full glittery Princess Leia drag—the classic white dress and bilateral brown hair buns. So awesome. The rest of band included short keyboardist Yoda, tall guitarist Luke Skywalker (white robe, Tattooine getup), and X-Wing fighter/drummer Luke in the orange-jump suit. St. Lucia's incredibly glorious take on *Star Wars Episode IV: A New Hope* was fucking awesome and I was in love with the band that much more. The ten-year-old in me that screamed bloody murder when ripping open a Millennium Falcon toy on Christmas morning had me screaming in the Roseland Theater.

---

38   Nerdgasm: When one experiences subsequent events of nerdiness, fandom, or geekiness that causes a sensory overload, loss of bodily functions, and a climax deep within the brain, in the section that recognizes specific information concerning comic books, occult television shows, video games, or electronics that only a specific section of the population would actually know about. Reference https://bit.ly/2mpkTtt

Josh and I about lost our minds when St. Lucia finally got to their most popular song *Elevate*. I hadn't jumped that much since the last Timbers match/win at home, pre-break-up. Who needs ecstasy or MDMA when you have friends, beer, a cute guy grinding on you, and *Star Wars*-themed musicians busting out amazing beats at a classic venue about to burst at the seams with dancing costumed people? It was easily the most fun I've had on *any* Date, with myself or otherwise, in recent memory.

After the concert, Josh and I parted ways. He said he had friends he was going to meet up with. He didn't "not know anyone in town" after all. I didn't take it personally, for the most part. I was on a personal and musical high. We hugged and said, "Don't be a stranger!"

We never met up ever again, but it didn't matter to me. I remember my face hurting from smiling so much.

Grunge Dorothy skipped back up Burnside Street with her friends to find the Emerald City and a stiff gin and tonic.

November 4th 2014—Election Day—This January would mark five years of my independent living in downtown Portland. In some ways it blew by, but more of it felt like just the amount of time it had been, full of things possibly expected for a woman transitioning from early twenties to late twenties, whatever that means (See Appendix A, Articles). Anyhow, during this period I had stood in front of this iconic building a bazillion times but never walked inside.

No. 17
Tour Pioneer Courthouse

The center of downtown, or mecca of public transit, is known as Pioneer Courthouse Square, or fondly, Portland's Living Room. Originally, the once grand Portland Hotel stood where the "brick lawn" now opens behind the second-oldest courthouse in the West. After the hotel was demolished in 1951, a two-story parking garage took its place. Between then and 1974, the business community fought over what should be done with the central block, eventually leading to its purchase by the City of Portland, an international design competition, and a plan for an open space coupled with a city-wide effort of brick-buying to sponsor its construction. April 6, 1984 the Square opened. My grandfather's name is on a brick somewhere.

Now the site of weekly events and gatherings, Pioneer Square is a sign of home to me as much as the funky carpet inside the Portland Airport[39] or my grandmother's old backyard in the Parkrose neighborhood. It is a red brick and stone "lawn" opening up behind one of the oldest-standing buildings west of the Mississippi, Pioneer Courthouse, which opened in 1875. It is a functioning courthouse, albeit for only five weeks out of the year I was told, but it is the top tier of the Ninth Circuit Court of Appeals; the next level up is the Supreme Court. The Ninth Circuit is the largest in the judicial system, covering Oregon, Washington, California, Idaho, Montana, Nevada, Arizona, Alaska, Hawaii, Northern

---

39   Portlanders are hilariously emotionally attached to the airport carpet, so much so that it was the grand marshal of a big city parade. https://bit.ly/2korLXn

Mariana Islands, and Guam.

I took the MAX[40] train to the transit mecca. The weather was cold and rainy, and I was glad to have an indoor activity for the day. After dropping my election ballot off in the gigantic dropbox sitting atop the brick living room, I pranced down the steps, crossed 6th Avenue, and walked up to the Courthouse entrance—which I had never thought to walk up to before my List was born.

The doorman gave me a quick lecture on the history of the building (see previous paragraphs) and told me what rooms I could and could not enter. Avoid the closed doors was the gist. Three judges had offices in the building, but the majority of it was a museum.

I took my time, not reading every poster full of lengthy historical explanation, but many of them. I thought the courthouse visit was a most appropriate way to celebrate women's suffrage, other than actually voting. I made it all the way to the top of the cupola for a 360-degree view of… more buildings. But once upon a time, you could see both the Willamette River and the West Hills, and every dirt road and wooden house in between. The pictures of what the view looked like from the late 1800s to mid-1900s were neat to compare to the current views of Niemen Marcus, the new Park Avenue tower being built behind it, the Galleria Mall, and other downtown monikers.

It's funny, Portland is not known for tall buildings, but the vertical concrete growth from farmhouse to penthouse in these old photos posted next to the ancient windows was stark.

By the time I started walking home in the signature Pacific

---

40   Metropolitan Area Express

Northwest rain, it was a bit after 3 p.m. As I wondered about the current ballot issues (marijuana legalization and GMO labeling) versus ballot issues from when the Courthouse was first built[41] (the Courthouse was open thirty-seven years before women could vote in Oregon) I decided I deserved a beer to end the educational Date with myself. You know, toast to Susan B. Anthony, Abigail Scott Duniway, and all the others who tirelessly worked so I could one day drop off my ballot and buy myself a beer at a local tavern without fear of prejudice, arrest, controversy, or my husband beating me.

I planned to have one microbrew and head home.

Oh, the silliness The Corner Bar has to offer, even on a Tuesday afternoon…

Side Story #5
The Singles' Mixer-Upper

So Marie walks into a bar at three o'clock on a Tuesday afternoon and the bartender says…

"Hey, just so you know, at six o'clock we're having a hundred people show up for a thing."

First off, ummm thank you for thinking I'm really going to sit here and drink for three more hours on a Tuesday afternoon. Honestly, my honest-to-God intent was to get a beer and walk home to finish whatever things were on my Shit-Needing-To-Get-Done-Today list.

---

41   Historical results of the 1911 city-wide election show narrow passing of a measure to fund street cleaning and strong support of funds for building police headquarters, a jail, and an emergency hospital. It also shows a strong rejection of measures to create pensions for police and fire personnel, approve salary of the city attorney, and prohibit the construction of wooden fences over eight feet. Reference https://bit.ly/2kEk13H

"Oh, I don't plan to stay that long, but out of curiosity's sake, what's happening later?" I asked the familiar barkeep.

"It's a Match.com Singles' Mixer," he says to me. "Something like ninety-plus RSVPs."

Interesting…go on…

"Hey, you know," he says wiping a glass clean, "we hosted one here a few weeks ago and it was pretty successful."

"Really?" I asked. He had my attention now.

"Yeah, in fact," he eyed me with a glint of match-making glee, "We had some girls at the bar before the last one and they stayed to check it out. They did really well! In fact, I think they did better than the poor people who signed up for the event. You should stick around, might find yourself someone."

Flabbergasted, I looked at my current appearance. I did not dress up for the Date with myself to the Courthouse: faded jeans, my brown walking shoes, a V-neck shirt, minimal makeup, definitely-not-brushed hair in a ponytail, and the peeling remnants of my fake arm sleeve tattoo from Halloween which was still stuck to my arm.

"I dunno, maybe I should go home and change clothes first," I halfway joked. I could be back in under fifteen minutes.

"Nah you look fine. You look good!" He smiled.

"Well, really I could go home, I have like no battery left on my phone," I set my smartphone down.

"Here, use my charger," he said, hooking up my phone. "Just hang out, drink your beer," he said. Well, he seemed to believe something amazing might happen.

As an avid bar-goer, I have learned it wise to listen to your bartenders. When in doubt, do what they say; they are way more sober than you. And if my bartender is telling me to stay and wait for hot single men to come talk to me, then by God, *I ain't goin' home.*

I went to the ladies' room. I finger-combed my hair and sniff-checked my armpits. I at least rinsed my mouth with water and found a stray mint in my purse.

I returned to the bar and spent the two hours catching up on Sports Center news. That, and watching the two old geezers in the back play Lotto games got me through to 5:45 p.m.

A young woman in a dress carrying a box showed up, presumably Mrs. Match.com. She set up nametags and sign-in sheets. Then people trickled in, non-regular Corner Bar people. Legitimately verified singles.

Okay, here we go.

I sat upright on my barstool, trying to look casual yet also alluring. Like writing, this is a skill I have yet to master but practice often.

Singles made their way around to the smiley lady in a dress introducing herself as the Match.com representative. When about the tenth person showed up right around 6 p.m. I noticed a repeating theme…something was…something was a bit unexpected…

A man (celebrity casting Donald Sutherland), wearing a horribly loud black-and-white print collar shirt that should be buttoned up at least one more notch, approached me at the bar.

Oh God, here we go…

"Hi there! You…you look too young to be here," he said to me, curiously.

"What, in a bar?" I asked, laughing.

"No, for the singles' mixer. It's the age fifty-five plus

group."

OOOHHHHHHHHHHHHH.

Wow…My face = priceless.

I looked at my not-so-trusty barkeep overhearing this conversation. He gave me a pleading look and mouthed, "I'm so sorry! The other one was with younger people!" I couldn't help but snigger. I slapped my palm down on the bar, and said to the gentleman, "No, I'm not here for the mixer, but I'll be rooting for you—from over *there*." I pointed to the other side of the bar which had a nice view of the awkward event. Near-retirement singles put on nametags and took playing cards. I guessed the icebreaker game involved finding people of your same suit.

Aside from the gigantic mix-up—*Oh my God, I stayed in the bar three hours for this, ha!*—it turned out to be a fun night. A few of the regulars popped in and we sat there betting on who would get lucky and pair up before the night's end. Also, I got a helluva party-pleasing story, banking this gem right above Side Story #6.

(You jerks, you're skipping ahead aren't you.)

No. 6
Take a Tai Chi class

November 6th, 2014—Another new month was upon me. Another turn of the calendar. Another thirty days of Rebooting in front of me.

Forward progress. Onward.

Taking a Tai Chi class has been on my general things-to-try list for a long time. It was something I never got around to.

In my research to find a beginner class, I found the Taoist Society offers first-timer classes only so often, and they teach each pose in sequence the traditional way. The man on the phone said, "It takes a few weeks to learn, and a lifetime to perfect." They had multiple locations and class times but I was never able to make it. (I must be busy or something.) This cool November morning I had the time and willpower to get off my couch, wanting to get my body moving.

The ever-informative internet spat out a hippie venue in my area called Vibrant Studio. According to the website, the studio offered classes in yoga, belly-dancing, music, clinics in Ayurvedic medicine, and Tai Chi. I signed up for a class and headed over.

The building, as I remember it, used to be a coffee shop at one point, and then unoccupied, but I liked what the new owners did with the place. Open, lots of light from windows, and a small studio space with a few solitary mirrors. For today's Tai Chi class, I was the sole participant under the ripe age of seventy, aside from the class teacher Fred (celebrity casting Fred Armisen). He introduced himself to me sweetly and we chatted about my history in dance, my List of Dates, and so forth. The other class participants, three elderly, openly-homosexual gentlemen, introduced themselves to me quite graciously.

We first stood in a circle. Fred began with basic movements. The three men had obviously taken Tai Chi before, but they humored me with the elementary review. I moved my hips back and forth in a figure-8 like motion, then added in arm motions ever so slowly. I learned the rudimentary purpose of each motion, and then tried to connect one to the next, eventually becoming fluid-like. After a few repetitions, we dove right into the sequence, which I learned was the same sequence first brought to the United States from China. I liked that about Tai Chi; that anyone can come together who knows the movements and they can just do it because they already know it. Kind of like Catholic Mass, without the guilt and tithing. Kind of like a dance, but less celebratory and more concentrated, like martial arts. Those YouTube videos of a thousand Chinese doing Tai Chi in Beijing stood out in my mind. Not quite as powerful in the tiny room with a view of lower Jefferson Street, but it did take my mind elsewhere for a while.

I fumbled as I tried to mirror the four others as best I could. Much of the movement was repetitive like yoga and I caught on eventually, with poses having names like Craning Serpent, or something like that. After forty-five minutes I asked each of them how and why they got into doing Tai Chi. For Fred, it was his calling. For the other three it was a combination of Tai Chi being exercise without joint damage, cardio without the long distance, mental release without the psychiatry bill, and companionship without the talking. I liked what they had to say. On my way out, while I put on my shoes and raincoat, I browsed the studio's other class offerings noted colorfully on a wall-length chalkboard.

I wondered what Thursday's "Wild Woman Dance" class was like and whether or not clothing was optional.

No. 30
Attend the Portland Opera

As a birthday present, my brother Topher (Topher Grace) and his wife Natalie (Natalie Portman) bought group tickets to the Portland Opera. I know, there's a lot of arts programs on my List, but if I want to call myself a legitimate appreciator, I feel the need to have supported at least all the major professional companies in the city. The Opera was opening their 50th anniversary season and decided to mark it with the reproduction of their first show *Die Fledermaus* by Johann Strauss II — originally performed by the company in the Madison High School Auditorium in 1964.

I had never been to the opera. I arrived at the Keller Auditorium ready to be dazzled. It was hoity-toity red carpet night for opening weekend. Everyone was dressed for a high societal affair. Topher showed up in his dapper suit and Natalie followed with a beautiful dress and shawl, holding her grandmother's antique opera glasses. Our younger brother Andy couldn't make it so our aunt Melissa happily took the fourth ticket.

Our group photo was taken on the red carpet before entering, and we found our way to the orchestra level seating. Though the opera was sung in English, subtitles scrolled across the top of the proscenium so we could follow along. I sort of wished for the original German, remembering my collegiate choir days, but it was wonderful nonetheless. I was surprised at how much dialogue there was in-between singing. A truly professional production, amazing those human beings can make music like that with just air and muscle.

Taking myself to the opera was quite a splendid evening, if I say so myself. Now to retire to the smoking room for a cigar and a brandy…

No. 36
Go to a University sporting event

I've covered my personal genesis of love for sports, right?

November 13th, 2014—So, it's a frigid day. I've dug out my supply of gloves, hats, and scarves. Christmas lights are starting to pop up all over town. Looking at my window A/C unit that I never took out because it's too damn heavy, I decided a Date with myself would be indoors. Elsewhere.

The Portland State University Athletics webpage showed free concessions at that night's women's volleyball game. Sold.

I couldn't remember the last time I physically witnessed a volleyball game, maybe the seventh grade? I thought, *Awesome, this is great!* I often find women's sports to have more grit than men's sports. Sure, anatomically men are stronger in some areas, maybe men can move faster and fly higher statistically, but women—they have survival instinct. Prowess. In athletics, that can be addicting, to watch or experience. This has led me to purchasing season tickets to the Portland Thorns—the city's National Women's Soccer League team—in addition to my season tickets to the Portland Timbers (Major League Soccer). What can I say, each summer I go on a considerable soccer-watching binge.

As I mentioned before, sports and competition have

always been an integral part to my family and my childhood. To this day, it is difficult to separate holidays from sports in the MacMillan household. There's always a football or basketball game on the TV in the background of family gatherings.

My dad was an avid high school and collegiate athlete at a tiny Division I school. He played baseball, lived at home, and commuted to class. The story goes: "All I got out of Calculus was a B and a wife!" My mother was a math major. She went to nearly every[42] college baseball game my dad played in for four years. Some of my earliest memories are of watching my dad play in alumni games, and then playing Barbies with my sister Aubrey (celebrity casting: Aubrey Plaza) on a blanket close to a baseball or soccer field in northeast Portland where my brother Topher played peewee. I remember our youngest brother Andy (Andy Samberg) being dragged to a bunch of my and Aubrey's dance competitions in high school. I remember going to many of Andy's senior high school basketball and football games the year I moved back to Oregon. Topher's kids came to a few games and now we go to their youth league events—and the cycle starts all over.

I will always associate spectating sporting events with family, which is why I felt so awkward going to this collegiate game alone when I had zero ties to anyone involved, at all. Why was it even on my List of 50 Dates, you ask? Because I live right by the school and I'll watch pretty much any sporting event.

After paying for my adult entrance fee—*No, not a student, thanks though*—I grabbed free popcorn and a Coke and made

---

42   My mom missed the one game when my dad hit a grand slam. This is unfortunately mentioned from time to time during holiday gatherings if the topic of baseball arises.

my way up to the green stands on the Home side of the gym. I picked a spot up high, behind a large group of people all wearing the same dark green jersey with the last name *Barrymore* emblazoned on the back. They were all chatting animatedly and taking photos, getting their encampment set up. Reading the program, I learned this was the Senior Game and that one (celebrity casting) Drew Barrymore, senior center, was the captain. I figured this must be her last home match in her college career and her entire family came out to support.

The match had a raucous start, the Lady Vikings taking an early lead. The Barrymores yelled and cheered. Many a "Let's go, Drew!" came from our section. I figured not only immediate but extended family had to be there. Four girls looking like Drew's sisters sat in a row, boyfriends in tow; I thought Drew had to be the baby. Mom and Dad sat near the front, and others looking to be their age, likely aunts or uncles; what I guessed was grandpas from both sides sat next to each other, shaking hands, comparing *Barrymore* jerseys. In-between sets, the sisters shared smartphone pictures, Dad took photos with a legitimate camera; the uncles went to talk with the grandpas. Mom talked with everyone, like moms do, and I sat a row behind all of them, watching with interest.

The name Barrymore rang a bell in my head. I saw on the game program that Drew was an alumna of my dad's high school. Assuming the rest of the family attended, I texted Dad to see if he remembered the family. Of course, he did. He could name every one there. He went to high school and college with an uncle, and Grandpa apparently was a big athletic program donor. There was an entire college dormitory named after Barrymore. It was apparent the

Barrymore clan stuck together like glue, and there was no question who on the court belonged to this tribe. I nodded my head in assent, smiling and knowing.

I knew this. I knew what this was. I had lived it many times. I looked at the Barrymores, one big vibrant/loud/supportive/crazy/unique family, fervently thinking:

That is what I want. That right there.

I can still hear my mother's voice (again, celebrity casting Sally Field), explaining sternly to one of us adolescent kids complaining about being dragged to yet another brother's or sister's sporting event— "You go to your siblings' games! It's just what you do!"—like we were clearly psychotic to even consider another option. It's the kind of concept I grew up with and wanted to pass on to my progeny, assuming I'd ever have any. I so profoundly wanted that in my life, as I told ex-boyfriend Dufus months ago.

Does everyone grow up to want what they had as kids for their own offspring? Is that just what happens when you become an adult? I hear you turn into your parents, but I'm not sure I believe that fully. I certainly look (and sometimes act) just like my mother and have my father's despicably charming wit, but that doesn't mean I'm going to photocopy their life and decoupage it onto mine—right?

Is this what I wanted because I thought I was *supposed* to want it?

Why couldn't I be happy with all the things I already had? I mean I was, and am, generally happy, but why did I want *more?*

Why couldn't I be satisfied with just dating until the time *was* right?

Did I really, maybe, bring up marriage and family too

soon to Dufus?

Was it really that ridiculous to want these things?

Was it really ridiculous to ask the man I loved for the things I wanted?

Was I stupid for believing him when he said he wanted them too?

Why didn't I want to be ultimately alone? It's certainly easier. I've lived alone successfully for five years, why not fifteen more? Why didn't I desire an endless solo adventure across the globe with no strings attached?

Is the grass always that much greener on the other side?

Existential wonder swirled around in my head as I watched the volleyball get bounced and slammed back and forth over the net. More cheers and jeers from the Barrymores.

I already have strings—I thought, to *my* cheerleading family.

I imagined the MacMillan clan here in this gym instead of the Barrymores (warning, more celebrity castings): me, Topher Grace, Aubrey Plaza, and Andy Samberg here to watch our imaginary fifth sibling, baby sister Drew Barrymore. Topher's wife Natalie Portman and my niece and nephew would be here. Aubrey's boyfriend Russell Brand would be here. Andy is too cool for a girlfriend, but he might bring some of his fraternity brothers. My parents Sally Field and Bill Murray would certainly be front and center, and dad's sister Melissa McCarthy would come, as she also played college sports. My mother's sister Julianne Moore and her husband Tom Hanks might drive up for it as well, and their two girls, my cousins Ariana Grande and Greta Gerwig. My grandmothers, Joan Rivers and Rosemary Clooney, would be there in spirit.

I suddenly realized Dufus did not fit in. I couldn't

comfortably put him there in the mental image. In more than two years, he came to only one of my rec league flag football games, memorably reluctant. He might come to this theoretical family volleyball event, but probably late after finishing whatever else was more important than fitting into my picture. I clearly didn't fit into his. That wasn't theoretical.

Empty fucking picture frame, Marie.

The Lady Vikings won the match after three exciting sets. The Barrymores hooted and hollered some more. As I got up to exit, hesitant to leave the warmth of the familiar scene even though it was not my own, I'd already answered some of my own questions.

I'd rather be sitting in a gym, with people who possibly annoy the shit out of me but whom I love anyway, because I know they'd show up for me. They show up for each other all the time, and knowing that is a priceless feeling that is definitely not ridiculous to want for myself and my own family.

I sauntered home after the game in the icy cold, alone, but comforted by the secure knowledge that it's okay to want what I want; and it is okay to ask for it. It's never not okay to ask for it from the people, or person, I love.

I fit just fine into my cheering section, and if someone else (i.e. a grownup man) comes along that fits into it too, awesome. If not, there's no rhyme or reason in walking away from my people to go find someone else. Besides, the game is just about to get good.

Part 3

The next twelve Dates

"I attribute success to this: I never gave nor took an excuse."

— Florence Nightingale

No. 10
See an indie film at NW Film Center

November 14th, 2014—Finding indie film screenings in Portland, Oregon is not exactly difficult, but I've walked past the NW Film Center hundreds of times and never made use of it. Back in August, I saw a great indie film called *Redwood Highway* at the Living Room Theater in the West End of downtown, but I decided to be stingy and not count it because it wasn't at NW Film Center. As you may have gathered, I really like movies. I'm really just a nerd for storytelling.

The 41st Northwest Filmmakers' Festival descended upon the Portland Art Museum for a few weeks. One Friday I was free, I decided to see a showcased collection of short films. Given that the majority of my film knowledge originates from feature-length films and blockbusters, I thought an hour and a half of ten-minute shorts would be cool and off the beaten path.

It was a popular night at the museum, $5 Fridays after

5 p.m. I purchased my festival tickets online ahead of time, and waded through people waiting in line to get into the museum for art's happy hour equivalent. The NW Film Center viewing theater was in the basement of the museum, yet again—another room/building/space I had walked past many times but had never gone inside.

The theater was sparsely populated; the shorts' showing was apparently the precursor to a major feature with a director Q&A so I had a feeling the room would fill up in about an hour. The organizers had us take ballots for scoring. I didn't do this, mostly because I couldn't see the ballot in the dark and they didn't bring up the house lights in-between shorts.

What I do remember is that I disliked the short films with dialogue. I found them annoying, like ringing in my ears. Who cares what they're saying? This was going to be over in a few minutes. I'm no film critic, this was just my personal opinion, but I had a positive reaction to the shorts with musical backgrounds, human subjects, and vibrant visuals. (Are you getting this *RottenTomatoes.com*?)

One short, whose title escaped me afterward,[43] centered on a rural Cajun/Louisianan traditional festival called *Courir de Mardi Gras* or "Fat Tuesday Run" where drinking, costume-wearing, dancing and debauchery are performed by all; generally, a vulgar backwoods communal affair. The short film was shot in black-and-white and visually stunning. To me, it was a redneck apocalypse meets *Monty Python*, with bluegrass music, oozing muddy, messy, liveliness. It was something deep and human. How can you get all those feelings in ten minutes? Well done, filmmakers, well done.

---

43   The short film was titled *Rougarouing*, directed by Michael Palmieri and Donal Mosher. Watch it on Vimeo here https://vimeo.com/61866298

Afterward, I daydreamed my way out of the museum. I imagined a short ten-minute film centered on a young female subject, with a long List of Dates with herself. It's cheesy montage time!—Cut to flashes of kayaking, Tai Chi, hiking, yoga and dance classes, cooking stuffed tomatoes in a pan, an inflatable donkey soaring in the air on a snowboard, cornhole tossing, shooting an arrow from a bow over a campfire, telling jokes into a microphone, watching a *Streetfighter* match on a gigantic projector screen, and thousands of naked bike-riders, all followed by different colored pens permanently crossing off each Date with purpose. St. Lucia's *Closer Than This* plays in the background.

I envisioned the young woman holding the now completed List—made delicate by repeated folding and accidental coffee spills—framing it behind glass, and hanging it on her apartment wall.

How I get there is the mysterious and entertaining part.

November 25th, 2014—I was feeling particularly productive. I checked off three Dates in a span of nine hours. *Woooohoooo!!!!!* I am woman, hear me roar.

No. 12

Go on a bike ride (a.k.a. confront your fear of riding a bike)

It's not so much being on a bike, or falling off a bike, that I am fearful of. In Portland, the majority of city roads have demarcated bike lanes. However, seeing people come into the hospital due to traumatic accidents means I know that thick white painted line on asphalt does not magically protect a bicycle from an automobile, no matter how experienced either driver or cyclist is. I think I would mind less if I took a bike out to a dedicated bike trail outside the city, but still I'd be moderately afraid. Part of it is fear of looking like an idiot, only part of it is falling off. I haven't spent time on a bike since I was probably ten years old. I know—shocking coming from a native Portlander. I live close to many downtown venues I can walk to just as easily…also, because…ALRIGHT, FINE! I'm afraid of falling off a bike.

However, it comes to No. 12—in the middle of winter no less. In preparation for this, I took one bicycle from my dad's collection. My dad adopted long-distance cycling in his middle age in place of a younger marathon-running version of himself. My new, scary wheeled possession was older, dark green and grimy, but it fits my lanky body. It was missing reflectors and lights, so I planned to adventure during daylight hours.

Sigh, groan. Uggggghhhh, just fucking do it.

I strapped on the free helmet I took home from a kids' helmet drive I volunteered at, hiked up my jean pants so they wouldn't get caught while riding, and put a water bottle in the special bottle holder on the old green monster. I made an underwhelming plan.

Bike 0.8 miles to No. 8.

Like a complete jerk, I stuck to sidewalks, and I couldn't have picked a more jerkoff time to ride a bike on the sidewalks. PSU classes had just got out and students switched between buildings in a timely fashion. I veered and swerved between people, with my helmet and hiked up jeans, sped up through the pedestrian area in the Park Blocks and continued up the middle paved path, past the Abraham Lincoln statue, and stopped at the Oregon History Museum. No doubt, I drew ire from everyone around me on foot.

I was sweating, more from nervousness and extreme self-consciousness than exertion. I strapped my helmet to my small leather backpack, like the rest of the bicycle people do, and parked my bike outside the entrance. It occurred to me then that I didn't have a bike lock, but since the requirements in No.12 were fulfilled I decided I didn't even care if someone stole it. I made it 0.8 miles and didn't fall off or get hit by a car, person, or flying object, or cry. I could probably do that again…I'd need to get the bike home somehow.

Fear confronted, not conquered, but whatever. Done and done.

For now…

No. 8
Visit the Oregon History Museum

I left my bike outside the museum entrance in a corner hidden from the street, hoping to deter the infamous daylight bicycle thieves. I showed the entrance volunteer my driver's license[44] and walked up the steps to the third floor, starting at the top and making my way down.

In the five years I've lived downtown, I've made several visits to the Portland Art Museum, but never to the History

---

44   The Oregon History Museum is free to Multnomah County residents. If you are one, please check it out. It's also free for everyone under 18, and $5 for everyone else. https://ohs.org/museum/

Museum across the street from it. Unlike the Art Museum, the History Museum is free to all Multnomah County residents. I can thank my unnervingly high city taxes for the cultural opportunity.

The third-floor permanent exhibit consists of the history of the State in general; from the first human inhabitants, different native clans, to the Lewis and Clark expedition, the Oregon Trail, Gold Rush and lumber exploits, right up through World Wars I and II and modern day society, highlighting a focus on green initiatives and city planning.

I really enjoyed myself. I took my time. I felt like I was immersing myself in my own family history in the West as I went along chronologically from one end of the exhibit to the other.

I don't have any Native American ancestry that I know of, but the MacMillans have been in the Oregon Territory for a long time now. My great-grandfather William MacMillan was U.S. Marshal after Oregon gained statehood. William carted his five kids, the youngest being my grandmother, and his Irish bride all over Oregon Territory, from Sitka, Alaska to Warrenton, Oregon—where my grandmother was born. I remember her telling me that to get to Portland they needed to take a river boat down the Columbia River. Eventually, my grandmother and her four older siblings settled in and around Portland.

William's father Donald, my great-great-grandfather, came to America from Scotland. According to surviving records, he and his wife Agnes arrived in New York circa 1865. I'm not sure how they travelled all the way to Oregon; it could have been in a covered wagon, but however they made it, I imagine it wasn't easy. In 2014, I had no grandparent, great-aunt, or great-uncle left alive to tell more stories from those years and century past. So, the History Museum became that much more enticing to me.

For those of you who do have grandparents still, call them up or bring them lunch. Do it today. They aren't going to be around forever, much less able to actually hear you or recognize you when you say, "Hey, Grandpa!" — "What? Who's there? Where are my hearing aids?"

Most of my deceased relatives lie interred at Rose City Cemetery, which my mother and I traditionally visit every Memorial Day weekend. The visit isn't stationary weeping like you might imagine. This ritual involves scrupulous cleaning and tidying up each burial site. We hedge with scissors, wash with water and granite cleaner, and place flowers and flags. It's a large amount of work as there are at least ten graves we visit. My mom has a map of all the family graves traced on a solitary scrap of paper, but its accuracy is debatable. We spend more time traipsing around graves in frustration looking for dead people we're related to than cleaning.

Other than the hilarity of us cussing at each other and pacing between rows of headstones, the thing I value most about this annual escapade is seeing and touching names ancient enough to have preceded the atomic bomb and women's suffrage, and then knowing I am connected in a very real and genetic way. It's a strange feeling. The oldest gravesite we visit at the cemetery is the upstanding tombstone of the aforementioned great-great-grandparents, Donald MacMillan and his wife Agnes, born in late 1840s died in early 1920s.

While reading excerpt after excerpt on the museum

walls detailing how hard life was on the frontier, it was Donald and Agnes I thought of, the life they had to forge so my great-grandfather, my grandmother, my parents, aunts, uncles, cousins, and now me and my siblings, could live on fearlessly. The take home quote from the museum was this:

> *People who do come must not be worried or frightened at trifles; they must put up with storm and cloud as well as calm and sunshine; wade through rivers, climb steep hills, often go hungry, keep cool and good natured always, and possess courage and ingenuity equal to any emergency, and they will be able to endure unto the end.*

–Elizabeth Wood, Oregon Trail, journal entry August 3, 1851, museum plaque

Hopping back onto my bike after the museum visit, I thought 0.8-mile ride home didn't seem so scary.

No. 9

Geek Trivia Night at McMenamins Kennedy School

A few years ago, I saw the development and then final production of Lauren Weedman's one-woman play titled *The People's Republic of Portland* at Portland Center Stage.

It was kooky and entertaining; always fascinating to see someone else come to know Portland through outsider eyes—and also Lauren Weedman is legitimately crazy and hilarious. Anyhow, in the stage production she regales the audience about going to the famed Geek Trivia Night without knowing anyone there, and being completely accepted into its nerdy splendor with arms wide open. I had heard of the legendary trivia event even before seeing her show. Dufus wasn't a geek at all (see Geek explanation in No. 24) and rolled his eyes at every *Star Trek* reference or R2-D2 sound I ever made; hence, one of many reasons why this epic Trivia Night made my List of 50.

I tried recruiting my siblings and nerdy friends to come participate, but I could only get one solid commitment. My friend Jewel (celebrity casting Jewel Staite) showed up at the popular venue a few minutes before I did. I received several panicky text messages from her before I could locate her in the busy auditorium and calm her nervous social anxiety. Also Nerd with a capital N, Jewel has knowledge stretching from *Dr. Who* to *Lord of the Rings* universes and has an Etsy store dedicated to geeky soap (think Han Solo in carbonite scented bars).

The two of us claimed chairs for our territory in Geekdom. I got a beer after a long wait in line (Jewel is a Shirley Temple gal) and we wrote our cleverly created two-woman team name down on our answer sheet: You Hyperdrive Me Crazy. Apparently, it was unwritten local tradition to come up with the craftiest team name of all time.

Setting the scene…

Imagine a gaming community, only ever knowing each other through audio via headsets, and then the same community of Nerds finally getting together in person, with beer, ready to aim and fire the kill shot at the rival group of Nerds sitting behind them on cushy couches and worn-down furniture in a converted elementary school gymnasium. An entire gym packed to fire-marshal capacity with adults happy to discuss their latest Renaissance fair adventure, comic book acquisition, continually lament *Firefly's* cancellation, or elaborate on their ever-evolving love/hate relationship with George Lucas. It was *The Big Bang Theory* cast but with more *Portlandia* flair, i.e. appropriate Stormtrooper T-shirts and but more beards and long-haired women holding babies in handwoven organic cotton bundles, whilst downing pints of IPA.

Geek Trivia was MC'd by two gents from a comic book store (duh, right?). They explained the rules—they are right unless the masses vote otherwise by calls of Yay or Nay, and tie-breakers are solved by a sudden death bout of the original mid-90s Nintendo game *Streetfighter* played on a massive big screen for all to enjoy.

Holy shit Batman, I'm not making this up. It was that awesome.[45]

As far as the two rounds of ten-question trivia, I estimate You Hyperdrive Me Crazy earned probably 40% correct, and that's generous. There were real players there, fresh out of their Nerd Caves for the night to dominate in heroic fashion. The top three teams tied with 100% correct plus bonus points.

My brother Andy showed up beer in hand just in time

---

45   Unfortunately, this was the second-to-last-EVER production of Geek Trivia Night at the Kennedy School. My brothers and I tried to make it in for the last session a month later, but alas, we were turned away. The gym had hit capacity 45 minutes prior to starting trivia, as there were that many people camping out for seats.

to witness the three-way tie-breaker. The crowd cheered as the gym lights went down and the projector flashed the grainy *Streetfighter* menu at the size of the gym wall. As a boy born in 1992 who has observed the digital evolution of N64 to smartphone games, Andy about died at the sight of this.

Familiar sounds of yelps and kicks and punches were accompanied by cheers and jeers from the community. Digital blood spurted across the screen with a second K.O.—and there was much rejoicing from the citizens of Geekdom. A champion had triumphed.

Balance was restored. The Dark Side had fallen. Link triumphed and Zelda was rescued. Captain Picard was no longer Locutus. Because, Gandalf the White.

Hey, some people juggle geese.

The ancients might say: *Vestra vexillum inusitus vola.*

Let your freak flag fly.[46]

No. 28
Take a yoga class

November 26th, 2014—This was an easy one. Yoga classes fall somewhere close to the "New York City: taxicabs; Portland: farmer's markets" analogy.

Some people are religious about their yoga practice.

---

46   This Date No. 9 became the inspiration for a six-part movie party series I hosted in 2015 entitled *Drunken Star Wars and Other Ridiculousness*. An anticipatory celebration of the impending release of *Star Wars Episode VII: The Force Awakens* in December 2015, it became a bimonthly gathering involving watching Episodes I-VI in story order (not chronological theatrical release) accompanied by themed cocktails (i.e. *The Anakin Chaiwalker*) and nerdy antics like trivia quizzes and drinking buzz words. Be forewarned, DO NOT choose "the Republic" as a drinking buzz word for Episode II unless you are prepared for a next-level hangover not even the Force can alleviate. See Appendix B for drink recipes. You're welcome, Nerds.

Through my dance training I've learned many yoga poses from different instructors' warm-up routines, but I can't say I've ever taken more than one official yoga class. I had to see what this was all about and pick up a few new poses for my personal workouts.

A popular studio in Northeast Portland had a new customer special that looked doable. I showed up for their basic Vinyasa afternoon class. It was cramped, lots of practitioners there—possibly fifty people in a space where you could not move four inches in any direction without bumping someone else's mat or extended limb. I was one of three people who raised my hand to indicate it was my first time at the studio.

I did learn new tricks and stretches, fodder for my no-gym-membership home workout routine. We used foam bricks for assistance with poses, something I had never tried but I'm sure a few friends would pay to get their hands on a video of me attempting. At times awkward, overall it was a neat class. Although, mentally I had trouble zoning out the other class takers.

The middle-aged man next to me with snake tattoos had quite the breathing technique (Read: *really fucking loud*). I thought he might give birth at any moment. Additionally, any time we reached our arms up to the sky I got a great view of everyone's armpit forests, a reminder to myself of where exactly I fell on the hippie spectrum—90% of the class consisted of women and only 5% shaved. This and the occasional dreadlock sweeping across my sweaty hands planted on my mat reminded me why I don't have a gym membership. I don't like other people watching me work out. I don't like being around other people when they work out. That's $50 a month I would rather spend at a spa (See No. 13).

Did I think of that while paying for the class on my way out? No, I got sucked into the monthly deal of, "for only five dollars more you can attend as many classes this month as you want." Well when you put it that way…

Did I attend any more classes in the next 30 days? Nope. I signed up for one but never made it. December got holiday-busy as usual. Despite my chagrin, yoga class was not altogether a useless experience. I have been working on that *natarajasana* pose in my living room. I figure I can have some *namaste* in my life and continue shaving my armpits regularly.

No. 37
Tour a brewery you haven't toured yet

At the conclusion of the 2014 calendar, Oregon's craft brewery count hit 220 different beer locales statewide, 83 in the greater Portland metro area. The state currently ranks #1 in number of breweries per capita and continues to lead the nation in percentage of dollars spent on craft beer.[47] Need I go on?

December 1st, 2014—Now I haven't been to all 220 breweries, but I estimate I have visited/drunk beer from at least one quarter of them. My friend Emma (see No. 35) and I were way overdue for happy hour. Instead of hauling out Christmas décor I decided to cross the interstate bridge before traffic could get preposterous, and spend the early

---

47   http://oregoncraftbeer.org/facts/

afternoon at a lesser known but impressive brewery in downtown Vancouver, called Loowit. I got their tasting selection, eight shot glasses of beer, and tested their merit while waiting for Emma to get done with work at her law office. The place was small and neighborhoody. While bar regulars talked with the one bar server I meandered through the back parts of the brewery, looking at the tall metallic mashtuns and marveling at their weird collection of arcade games. I guessed the brewmasters had to stay entertained in-between sessions of fermentation practice.

Emma eventually arrived and we shared pints while catching up on gossip and bitching about the universal shittiness of dating. Loud gesturing and scoffing at saved text messages from idiotic boys kept us going, to the utter annoyance of the regulars in attendance at the bar, I'm sure. No matter, Emma's "go fuck off" expressions kept them at bay. Emma is one of the most solid drinking buddies a gal could have.

We had the ongoing argument on the differences between fermented grapes vs hops vs anything else, debating how the atmospheres surrounding each can be so staggeringly different yet the creation process is pretty much the same. We planned plausible trips to Napa, and Europe, and the next bar we were going to. We planned the destruction of men who had done us wrong. We laughed like tipsy women do, cursed like drunken sailors do, and walked to the next bar like badasses do.

Another brewery close by in downtown provided more hoppy deliciousness—because why not? Dispensable income + high concentration of original beer taps = Marie's free time and wallet contents spent well and without regret. Cheers!

No. 2
Attend OMSI After Dark

December 3rd, 2014—The Oregon Museum of Science and Industry is a place I associate with second grade field trips and boring days of summer vacation when my mom could think of no other way to entertain us children at home. Since returning to my home state as a fledgling adult, I've gone to OMSI with my young niece and nephew to play in the kids' zone but haven't found another reason to visit. Despite this, OMSI puts on applaudable adult-centered programming following the ever-popular Portland equation of *beer + (X) = attendance*. Behold, "OMSI After Dark"—a night of scientific knowledge sprinkled with libation and merriment.

Tonight's theme: Fire and Ice.

Walking into the building, I immediately realized what a date night thing this was. Not in my solo sense of the term Date Night, in the hand-holding Couple's Night sense. Ah, well, whatever. I was there to stay and enjoy it I would.

On the heated side of things, fire was represented in a lecture on volcanic activity in the Pacific Northwest, a fire tornado demonstration, and a room full of salsa and hot sauce vendors with free samples. Conversely, cold beer was available for cash to wash down ghost-pepper levels of tongue-burning. They had a demonstration with dry ice, and the regular permanent exhibits were open to enjoy.

I walked around casually, not talking to anyone, taking in the science demos and eating nearly every available free sample. I felt like a solo skater at the roller rink who hasn't realized it's Couples Skate Only.

On an outdoor patio a wilderness survival station let you practice building a fire from scratch, roast marshmallows, and learn tips on not freezing to death outdoors. And of course, there was an archery station. Makes total sense, right?

I picked up the bow and shot down the stretch, missing the target completely; the arrow soared into the dark yard beyond. A volunteer had to run to retrieve it. Couples standing in line behind me stared impatiently as we waited for the guy to return with the arrow. I told them to piss off, with my eyes. I chugged the rest of my beer, still unable to get the hotness from multiple salsa dips to abate. I tossed the empty cup and pulled the arrow back into the bow again—*Couples Night my ass*, I thought—and let it rip.

I missed the target but I hit the arrow on the board. Practice makes perfect right?

No. 13

Spa Day. no seriously. spend most of the day there.

December 23rd, 2014—The year was coming to a close. Traditionally, I work a lot the last two weeks of December, filling in holes in the schedule so I can have the beginning of January free to recover from New Year's Eve parties and watch college football. This year was no different. I worked extra shifts and did my winter holiday duty of Christmas Eve and Christmas Day at the hospital. But in-between all the madness of wrapping presents in my scrubs on the floor of my living room, I found a day to utterly indulge myself.

I showed up at a moderately-priced downtown spa around 2 p.m. and didn't get home until 8 p.m. I threw down extra dollars for a ninety-minute massage, a sixty-minute facial, and a foot scrub plus shellac manicure and pedicure. I was able to reboot my body and squeeze out all the toxicity from the year, ready to spend the last of the calendar with perfectly polished nails, a bright clean face, and zero back pain. As someone who attends to the basic needs of really sick people for a living, I couldn't describe how amazing it was to be quiet for five hours, let someone else take care of me, release all my stress, anxiety, and tension. Filled with peaceful energy afterward I seriously considered climbing Mt. Hood and becoming a monthly spa member.

Okay, I ended up only doing one of those things.

For those of you who think this is the epitome of white girl bullshit, go get a professional massage and then tell me to fuck off.

No. 26
Find a meet-the-chef dinner

December 26th, 2015—This one was difficult to lock down. Foodies book out special dinners months ahead of time. My friend Cate is a foodie (See No. 15). She calls months ahead to book spots at Michelin-starred restaurants. In fact, she recruited me to help call a place in New York City at 7 a.m. Pacific time because that was the earliest anyone could reserve three months ahead, and everyone who ascribed to culinary exquisiteness would be trying to call at the same time. I hit Call on my phone eight times between 7:00 and 7:03 before I texted Cate that I had no luck. Anyway, pretending to be a foodie was a new experience for me.

Sometime in November, I found a local place that did community style dinners. I called and inquired about their December 26ᵗʰ traditional Italian night. The nice lady on the phone said they had room.

"Great! So, it's just me, by myself. How does the seating work? Will I be at a table all by myself or is it more community seating?" I asked nervously, not wanting to be sitting by myself for a five-course meal.

"Oh no, we kind of sit everyone down together at one big long table," Phone Lady told me, "You'll be fine."

"Awesome, I'm in. Thanks," I replied.

Fast forward to the night of. I put on a dress and heels. I curled my hair even. I looked fabulously polished thanks to the preceding No. 13. I arrived early. I walked around the building looking for the entrance. I could see through basement windows a few cooks hard at work preparing. My mouth was watering already. I strutted through large entrance doors, down a concrete hallway, and turned a corner to a lovely glass door that read *Simpatica Dining Hall*. I stepped through the doors and up to the hostess counter which hid the modest dining room behind it. The nice gal there checked me in and said, "Right this way."

My heels clicked on the hard floor following her a few feet away to—*damnit!*—my own table, set for one.

I ground my teeth as I sat down, expertly disguising my sincere disappointment. A few other parties of more than six people were already seated at some of the eight small tables scrunched together in the smallish dining hall.

Fuck. I have to sit here by myself and eat, quietly, for five courses.

Insert moderately silent self-pep talk as I crunched on

salted almonds beautifully arranged on a plate next to my water glass. A waitress appeared. "Just you tonight?"

"Yeeee-yep," I affirmed, as positively as I could.

"Okay then, let me go over a few things…"

She elaborated on the night's menu choices. Authentic Italian required wine pairings with each course. I elected for the Half Glass option because I was already spending a cash wad on this Date with myself. I think the two proficiently chic yet also spunky waitresses (celebrity casting: Ilana Glazer and Abby Jacobsen) took pity on my lonely table and upgraded me to Full Glass status no extra charge. I guess there were perks for going it alone.

After the first glass of wine I settled in fine. I overheard other guests' conversations, none worth mentioning, but then I decided no one was talking about me or pointing me out. They were all talking about the food or the wine or each other. I was invisible. I decided even if I wasn't, I'd have a cover story. Maybe I was a food blogger. Maybe I was food critic. Maybe I was elected the Sexiest Food Critic of 2014. Maybe I was a Public Health official investigating the use of organic "herbs" by the restaurant. Maybe I was a CIA assassin and my target was…*damn this wine is good.*

I reveled in the imaginative stories until the main dishes started coming out and I mostly forgot any remaining self-consciousness I held. To keep it short: the food was divine. The two chefs did a mind-blowing job putting together the menu. They came out to the dining room before the first course and explained the work they put in for each dish and where the ingredients came from. At the end of the five-course extravaganza one of the two chefs came to my table, shook my hand, and asked why I was there all by my lonesome. I told him I was on a Date with myself, that I'd never done anything like this dinner before, and wanted a chance to get dressed up and eat wonderful food.

He absolutely loved that, and told me to come back any time.

I had to wait a good amount of time after I paid my check, after the rest of the patrons left, and after Ilana and Abby starting sweeping the floors, before I felt solid enough to drive home.[48] I didn't plan on the Full Glass upgrade they bestowed upon me so I spent time chatting with them after dessert, guzzling ice water. I thanked them profusely. I imagined they were going off to an amazing rave party afterward to get high and make art.

Speaking of getting high, I was feeling pretty damn good about myself. That was not easy—sitting there all alone for a few hours, eating delicious food, conversing with no one but the servers. On the other hand, I felt fortunate to *not* have to listen to anyone else's bullshit. At least, I didn't have to endure others' problems and boring gossip while swigging Italian wines and trying to genuinely enjoy my handmade pasta and fresh-from-the-garden tomato sauce. I think I rocked the solo act with style.

Feeling so amazed at my composure, I took to the Corner Bar in my dress and heels (yes, people were astonished) for a nightcap—I didn't want to end the celebration.

You know how sometimes you want to bottle up a feeling and put it on a shelf for later? So you can open that bottle up, smell it and remember the feeling? I felt so incredibly sure of my own awesomeness that after not one, but two different

---

48   This is a world pre-Uber and Lyft in Portland. Well, before I would really embrace it as an acceptable, safe, and non-creepy form of transit.

hot guys gave me their phone numbers, I asked out a third adorable man sitting with a group of friends. I figured with those odds I wouldn't be alone on New Year's Eve. The first two hunks who gave me their numbers never met up with me sadly, but the last one I did go out on two dates with.

When in Rome, right?

Side Story #6
Cinderella Man

December 31st 2014—Every year since junior high school I've kept my New Year's resolutions written in a journal. Relatives and friends used to give me leather bound notebooks as gifts all the time because I had always kept a diary. During big family vacations I kept a journal detailing the quality of the hotel rooms my five family members and I crammed into, or later in my young adulthood I kept track of the different people and places I encountered while on a road trip. This particular New Year's journal is cloth-bound with a floral print, and I have a feeling one of my grandmothers gave it to me. Near the beginning of this journal, my "Goals, Wishes, and Hopes" for 2001 are inscribed. It was the middle of my 8th grade year, and the highlight of my goals that year was: "Have a totally awesome time at summer camp!"

Ah, youth.

Skimming over the last fourteen years' worth of goals proved quite the inspirational and hilarious experience. I could see where I checked off things like, "Go to Freshman Homecoming" and, "Apply to at least 3 colleges" and, "Write more." Most of the items over the years can be considered "check-off-able," and as the 2000s passed I wrote more goals and accomplished less of them. I'm not certain what this speaks to, perhaps the demanded excellence of my childhood bleeding into my adult independence, or the focus on accolades rather than experiences.

Obviously, as noted previously, I'm kind of a List person. This year I took this into account. I wrote only five solitary items under "Goals, Hopes, and Wishes" for 2015:

1.) Travel as much as possible

2.) Care less about accomplishment and more about savoring life's experiences—planned and unexpected alike

3.) Finish 50 Dates with myself. Maybe let someone read the journal of its crazy course

4.) Finish a play. Have a reading of it—in a living room or on a stage, doesn't matter

5.) Pay off college debt. Start saving money for… something

I always end the December 31st entry with a quote, a theme for the Year. This time I borrowed from the notorious Anonymous: "Sometimes when things may be falling apart, they may be falling into place."

I finished penning the above while getting ready to go out on the town to party. I love New Year's Eve. It's one of the better excuses to wear eye glitter. It turned out I did not secure a date, so I decided to wing it with Blake and her boyfriend Jake. The three of us, dressed to the nines, arrived at The Eleanor Rigby[49] before 9 p.m. to avoid the cover charge and get good seats. We landed prime real estate right at the bar. There was a champagne special of course. I couldn't

____
49   Not the actual bar name

tell you what I ordered to drink; my eyes were scanning the crowd for available, unattached, kissable men—because Marie was on the prowl. Like a lioness in the wild sniffing out her prey (insert jungle noises, lion growls), because she wasn't going to be that shoe-carrying, mascara-smeared, completely-hammered single girl whose lips wrapped around only a champagne bottle come midnight. She was gonna kiss someone beautiful, damnit.

Sorry, I'm not sure what came over me, referring to myself in the third person from the set of *Rambo,* but that's sort of what the beginning of that night felt like—a kind of out of body experience. I was quite determined to kiss someone; you know, erase all the badness from this year and launch successfully into the next. With Blake and Jake helping scout at my side (Jake: "That guy is alone." Blake: "Nope, girlfriend. See, three o'clock.") I ended up landing my eyes on him: Cinderella Man.

Tall. Athletic appearing. Dressed nicely. Holding a drink, scanning the crowd. Clean cut and put together, celebrity casting: Josh Charles. Standing next to him was a super good-looking shorter muscular man, celebrity casting: a short Anthony Mackie. *Damn, they're both hot.* Hell, I had a hard time choosing between the two. The lioness in me hesitated for only a moment. However, Cinderella Man took the prize because of his height. His friend was gorgeous, but much shorter than me, especially with me in heels. Sorry dude. I thought maybe Cinderella Man arrived at the ball looking for Princess Charming.

Well drink up, skippy, and get over there! It's 11:12!

I told myself, chewing on the tiny straw in my drink. By then the bar had filled up and there was a line around the block to get in for a cover.

I don't normally like this bar. I hate bars with covers. The Rigby is usually full of hipster kids who talk about how disgusting coal-dependence is *while* they smoke cigarettes. But tonight, everyone was up for the formal occasion. No skinny jeans or flat-billed hats accounted for, though sometimes I thought I was at an anorexic fashion show.

"Go, girl," Blake said to me, watching me stare at Cinderella Man.

"I'm going," I said, chewing on my straw still.

"Forty minutes," she added.

"Okay. Okay! I'm going," I said sucking down the last of my cocktail.

I slid my glass toward the bartender, whirled off my bar stool, and stepped around people trying to get that bartender's attention. As people moved toward the bar I walked away from it against traffic toward my goal. I made it about three feet before the thought occurred to me that Cinderella Man might be waiting for a date. I inwardly told my common sense to SHUT THE FUCK UP as I came within visual range of my target.

He smiled. I smiled, and died a little. I said hi. He said hi. And I died a little. Introductions were made. Then I found my rhythm: "So you guys here just by yourselves?" And they were.

Boom! That's how it's done.

I caught Blake and Jake giving me the thumbs up from the bar. I thought this was great, Midnight Kiss secured. Simple. But the more I talked to Cinderella Man the more fireworks shot out my eyes, the weaker my knees became, the less simple it became.

Cinderella Man told me he and his friend went to high school together—my dad's alma mater. *Okay, not a huge coincidence.* The two played football there together. *Cool, athletes, I dig that.* He just bought a condo—*Nice*—and works in financial something whatever—*Employed and stable, bonus*—has a huge family, grew up in the Parkrose neighborhood—*now that's coincidental*—his dad went to Parkrose High—*So did my mom!*—and his dad's parents just sold the house they had for over fifty years on this old street—*Wait, stop, hang on...*

I knew that street name, my grandmother had lived on it. We got out our phones and Google Mapped our respective grandparents' houses—which were only three houses away from each other. I swear it, true story. Our minds were blown. We were convinced his dad and my mom plus siblings ran around the neighborhood together, probably walked to the little dairy at the end of the road to get ice cream together, probably went to elementary school together, and definitely went to junior high and high school together.

Holy shit.

This can't be nothing. This can't mean nothing. (*God, I am such a girl.*)

By this time his friend Anthony Mackie had taken a cue and moved on to find his own entertainment. Cinderella Man and I marveled at the uncanny chances and we started getting more into personal interests. I casually glossed over my career goals and weekend rec league habits. I was already totally enamored with this dude when he dropped this sentence: "Well, if I could put down my truly greatest skill on my resume it would be catching a football."

Zoom—plant!—Arrow to my heart. My pupils morphed into Valentine shapes, and I thought: *I wanna date this guy.* Not,

I wanna sleep with this guy—or, I wanna go home with this guy—or, man I'd like to get beers with him sometime—but I WANNA DATE THIS GUY.

I can't explain the instantaneous desire to be this man's love interest. Maybe it was the unbelievable flukes, the need to find out if our parents remembered each other, our many overlapping sports interests, the size of his shoulders and dynamite smile, or maybe it was the fact that he wasn't unemployed/gay/homeless/wearing a bro tank (See Fig. 1). Thinking back, the alcohol was probably a factor. Anyway, it was the first time I had considered anything remotely close to emotional attachment since, well you know.

Sigh. Insert twinkly sound effects. Here comes the starry, fantastical Cinderella-goes-to-the-ball scene…

Before I realize it, the bar is counting down 3, 2, 1 and his lips are on mine—freaking magic, like a key change in a Mariah Carey song. He says, "Happy New Year. You ready to have a good time?" I nod and say something unintelligibly affirmative. I'm slightly afraid he might hand me Ecstasy.

Nope, no psychogenic drugs, but we party like it's 1999. A DJ starts busting out beats and a small dance floor appears. He buys me drinks. We dance. We make out some more. More magic. I accidentally leave my clutch purse on the bar and think I've lost it. Drunk Marie sees opportunity in this failure. I say to Cinderella Man, intentionally testing the waters, "Well if I don't find my keys, I guess I'm sleeping at your place."

"I'm okay with that," he replies, his hand on my ass. I don't care if I find my keys.

Soon after Blake and Jake find me on the dance floor, say they are leaving and ask if I am alright. I wave them off much too enthusiastically. They laugh and head out. The next time I swing by the bar the bartender hands me my clutch. I thank him, sort of. We dance more. His friend Anthony reappears with some girl, Amber (celebrity casting: Amber Tamblyn). Cinderella Man whispers to me about how he is good friends with Amber even though Anthony and Amber broke up recently, so there's residual drama from that but they're all cool with partying together…or something.

What? Okay, whatever, I don't care. I already have the invite to Cinderella's house. I'm drunk enough at that point to hug Amber and say "So nice meeting you," like fifteen times. The house lights come up; it's nearing 2:30 a.m. No one moves to leave, but it's still loud and there's lots of commotion. Staff members are trying avidly to kick everyone out. The four of us kind of sway back and forth waiting for our land legs to return. Cinderella isn't making a move and it is way past midnight. I look up at him and say something like, "Wanna hang out?"

Smooth, Marie, real smooth.

"What?" he replies, shouting. The place was so loud still.

"Did you wanna get out of here?" I ask, closer to his ear. He looks at me confused, blankly, like he still can't hear me. I shake my head and hold up my finger with a gesture like—*don't go anywhere I'll be right back*. I figure we could talk outside where we could hear each other.

I went to retrieve my coat from a pile of a hundred other winter coats. I had my clutch purse in hand. I came back with my coat folded over my arm and—

—(*looking*)—

—(*searching around*) —

—(*panic*) —

Not on the dance floor. Not closing his tab at the bar. Not at the door. Not in the bathroom. Not outside the bathroom. Not just outside the bar. Not sitting at one of the stupid picnic tables. Not waiting at a cab with the door held open. Not down the street. Not in the street. Not across the street. Not anywhere looking for me. Not anywhere.

I bust back into the bar past the bouncer who yells at me. The only people inside are staff members sweeping up the dance floor which is now abandoned. No glass slipper to be found, just an inordinate amount of broken glass being swept into trash cans. I saunter back outside and plop down at one of the picnic tables utterly stupefied and confused. Other drunken couples and groups are hailing taxis like it'll bring them winning lottery tickets. I watch the New Year begin in disastrous fashion, for a good twenty minutes, thinking:

Maybe they were coming back? Maybe he had to walk the other two to their car or something? Maybe the breakup drama exploded and he had to intervene? What did I miss? Was he really into that Amber chick the whole time? Was she actually his girlfriend and that drama story a cover up? Did he maybe have a wife? Was I just embarrassing? Was I too over-the-top into him? Did I read the ass-grabbing "come back to my place"-signals wrong? Was there something on my face?

I get out a tiny mirror from my clutch and examine my 3 a.m. appearance. *Nope. I don't see the shoe-carrying, mascara-smeared, completely-hammered single girl. I'm not holding a champagne bottle. We never exchanged phone numbers…in fact, he never asked…*

The plausibility has already dawned on me, but now it sinks in as fact.

That motherfucker left me alone at a bar at 3 a.m. on New Year's Day.

I could end the story there, really—it's not like this tale has a good ending.

After about twenty-five minutes sitting outside in the cold at one of the stupid picnic tables, I decided I needed to get as far away from that bar as possible. I got up, crossed Grand Avenue, and started walking over the Morrison Bridge. I followed a group of revelers on the pedestrian walkway. I did my best not to think about how Dufus and I walked across the Hawthorne Bridge after midnight carrying champagne bottles the last two NYEs after partying on the East Side. I did my best not to feel the most recent rejection, or the initial one.

When the walkway turned into a stairwell down to the Eastbank Esplanade I realized I'd be dodging after-3 a.m. drivers on the bridge if I continued. I didn't want to play life-or-death drunk Frogger at that moment, so I wrapped my coat around my waist tighter, crossed my arms, and threw my head up to the sky—*fuck it*. I turned around after letting out an infuriated screech. I hobbled back to the cursed bar to get a cab.[50] There was almost no one left there waiting for rides in the cold. I shared a taxi with a couple heading downtown. They got dropped off in the Pearl District and my fare was pretty cheap after that. When I got home I took off my heels and fancy wear and crawled into bed without taking off any makeup or brushing my teeth. I didn't care

---

50   Again, before smartphone app ride-sharing was a widely accepted form of transit. I didn't trust Uber or Lyft for a long time. I'd say, "Wait, you get in a stranger's private car, and just trust that that they are *not* going to drive you into the woods to maim and kill you?" Ironic really, judging by the trust I put in Cinderella Man.

about my mascara anymore so I did, in fact, cry.

I had become a pretty close resemblance of the mascara-smeared, completely-hammered single girl, weeping into her pillow with her heels thrown on the floor.

Later New Year's Day, I went over to my parents' house to watch college football and nurse my hangover. I mentioned the last name Charles to my mom, and the grandparents' house near the one she grew up in. She immediately remembered that motherfucker's family.

"Oh yeah, I've been in that house. Yeah! We totally ran around with the Charles kids," my mom said. With total embarrassment, I told her the story of Cinderella Man's evaporation without so much as an "I must go!"

Then what did my mother and I do? If you and the Internet are well-acquainted then you already know.

Google didn't provide much. Neither did Instagram. But I did locate Josh Charles on Facebook. We had one friend in common. *Shit.* Then I wavered. Now I had a way to contact him, but I also realized if I could find him *he* could find *me*. He did after all tell me to see if my mom remembered his uncles, and I told him to ask his dad if he remembered my mom. And yeah, I did check Missed Connections on Craigslist like a total loser.

As a few dates with other guys rolled around in early January (see end of No. 26) I could still not get Cinderella Man off my mind. I was mostly convinced he ghosted[51] on purpose, but I kept thinking, *what if???* Like any other person has and would in this situation, I came up with extremely ridiculous what-if scenarios.

What if he got hospitalized because of the bus that hit

---

51   Ghosting explained: https://bit.ly/1x2NcsG

him at 2:50 a.m. on January 1st?

What if his phone got stolen or broke and he's waited two weeks to replace it?

What if his car turned into a pumpkin?

What if he JUST WASN'T INTERESTED and didn't have the BALLS to SAY ANYTHING like EVERY OTHER GUY EVER? What if he's that unoriginal? What does that say about me?!

AHHhhhhhhhh goddamnit!

I couldn't decide whether to message the ephemeral Josh Charles on Facebook or not. I was so distracted by this to the point of not even listening to the new guys I was meeting up with on real dates; which is when I decided I needed professional advice. I conferred with my most trusted male advisors, my flag football mates. I told them the whole story, without sparing any detail so they could give me true insight. Our quarterback Kris (celebrity casting: NBA star Kris Humphries) said there was a miniscule chance something happened and maybe the guy didn't get around to sending a message yet because, simply, Josh Charles was an idiot.

"Just message the guy. If he doesn't respond then you have your answer, and you'll know he's an asshole a lot sooner than you would otherwise." Sage words, Kris Humphries.

So I did. And Facebook already had that super awesome feature where you can tell if the intended receiver has actually *seen* your message or not. Well, the infamous Josh Charles immediately saw my pathetic

Hey, it was fun meeting you on NYE at Eleanor Rigby, would love to get beers sometime if you're interested

message. He did not respond that day or the next.

Two days from then I got no words, but I got a Tiny-

Thumbs-Up symbol.

You know, that little thing that was situated right next to the Send Arrow in the message text box? —a symbol which I myself have hit by mistake instead of the send button.[52]

I read this awkward reply as either a.) A complete typo or, b.) Josh Charles was showing all his friends the message and laughing about the pitiable gross loser girl he met on NYE and how he decided that getting laid wasn't worth it as she embarrassed herself from here to Saturn and back. I imagined one of his many chuckling cronies accidentally hit the Tiny-Thumbs-Up reply button while handing his phone around to raucous banter about silly whores and drunken girls at bars. Oh God, I got Tiny-Thumbs-Upped. *Fuck my liiiife.*

Douchebag. Chicken-shit. Ignominious jerk…or maybe I was just that unappealing? Needless to say, my confidence was crushed.

People—guys and gals and persons across all gender spectrums—do the other person you're trying desperately to ignore a favor and just say: "Hey, sorry, I'm not interested." It'll save humanity a lot of heartache, data overcharges on cell phone bills, unnecessary calorie-consumption, Kleenex, Xanax, and reasons why we inevitably will say *piss off* to the next not-really-an-asshole person who genuinely wants our romantic attention.

I guess that's just a bit of bad Karma.

Josh Charles, yours is still coming.

---

52   See a screenshot at mariemacmillan.com/rebootphotos

No. 11
Take a cooking class

January 8th, 2015 — I know this is coming right after my gourmet meet-the-chef dinner but I didn't necessarily plan it that way. I reserved the cooking class ages ago at Portland Culinary Workshop, a class entitled "Cooking for One." Appropriate, right? Seriously though, it can be tough to shop for, prepare for, and store food for one single person. It's kind of an art form. The first year I lived alone I was terrible at this. There were a lot of instant meals, and boxes that read "just add water." Since then I've branched out and improved upon my simple culinary skills. I own a slow cooker now. I can make a mean meatloaf and totally badass chicken nachos. I don't buy dinner in a cardboard box anymore. I try to stick to the produce, deli, and meat counter sections at Fred Meyer grocery. However, this is an area where I will always have room for improvement.

For about $60 I reserved a spot at a hands-on group lesson. I took the Yellow MAX line out to North Portland and walked a few blocks to the workshop location. It was a cold but not frigid evening. I walked up to the space situated between several businesses, its front windows overflowed with massive aloe vera plants.

I arrived a few minutes late, but it didn't look like I had missed much. The instructors were completing introductions. Most of the 16-person class had not been to a workshop before, but a few were returning for additional fun. The lead instructor (celebrity casting Allison Janney) did a few short knife and cutting demonstrations, which I appreciated because I felt like I was slicing and dicing wrong all the time. She showed us where all the ingredients were laid out at each table, expertly arranged and labeled. Allison Janney and her assistants handed out printed directions, and we broke into two pairs per large table and electric stove. Every person got a large cutting board and knife.

The menu for the evening included Herb Roasted Chicken with penne pasta, pear, blue cheese, and sautéed mushrooms; Asian stuffed tomatoes and salad wraps; Squash fritters and mashed herbed squash; Arugula salad with pear, blue cheese, spiced nuts, and Dijon maple vinaigrette.

My mouth is watering rewriting the menu here. We started by stuffing the birds, and an assistant took them to a huge oven. Then while the chicken cooked, we chopped more ingredients and stuffed tomato halves. It was super fun and educational.

The class attendees varied considerably. Of the foursome at my table, my partner slicing bok choy and green onions directly across from me was a recently retired woman in her sixties just looking to get out of the house and try something new. The pair next to us included a younger guy, probably nineteen or twenty, with some sort of Asperger's syndrome, I guessed. He loudly claimed he knew a lot of these cooking techniques anyway but his mom made him sign up for the class to try to meet people besides his virtual Call of Duty friends. His cooking partner was a young professional dude with average looks and less than average height. He and I chatted about the intramural rec leagues around Portland and politely argued which has the best adult kickball.

Once the tomatoes were stuffed we used grapeseed oil to fry them. The room filled with white steam and loud sizzling noises. While I was using tongs to flip over a tomato half, a tiny bit of scalding oil splashed up onto my cheek. I reacted involuntarily and stepped back holding my face. I grabbed a wet towel to wipe it off and suddenly Allison Janey the instructor appeared holding a long, severed end of an aloe vera leaf which she pressed onto my face.

"There you go, dear," she said while holding my chin. Awkward; however, effective. I'm guessing this happens a lot to novice cooks, hence the forest of aloe vera in the front windows.

Approximately two hours after putting the chicken in the oven, a long table was set for a grand dinner. Giant bowls and pans displayed our successful culinary creations. The food was delectable, but the class was enjoyable too. I had the opportunity to use ingredients I'd never think to purchase, like cooking sherry and Thai basil, and I completely changed the way I use a knife. We ate somewhat quietly because we were all immensely enjoying the spread. I took home a whole box full of leftovers and the cooking handouts, and of course the knowledge. In the following weeks I purchased two new high-quality cooking pans and prepared several of the menu items again.

The Call of Duty kid followed me to the MAX stop after dinner, talking about living at home the whole time. I didn't mind so much—in a way, he was braver than I was. I figured this was much farther out of his comfort zone than it was mine.

No. 46
Take a solo road trip. Must be gone from home at least the whole day

February 5ᵗʰ-7ᵗʰ 2015—Back in November, I had this grandiose plan to drive to Central Oregon and experience Bend. I was going to try snowshoeing, or something on the mountain (No. 45), maybe see a play (No. 1), or find a hiking group (No. 4), and get some of the Ale Trail done (No. 37) in addition to No. 46's solo road trip. I had this mammoth strategy to check off several Dates in one weekend, but the weekend I hoped for ended up being the first big snow of the winter and all the roads over Mt. Hood were locked up. I didn't want to kill myself driving over the pass in my beat-up Jeep without all-wheel drive. I sadly cancelled my first Airbnb reservation, but the hosts reimbursed me 100% because the people staying in the lovely cottage at the time couldn't leave either because of the weather. So, the first snow of the winter killed my first Bend plan, which ended up being the last snow of the winter as well. The whole Northwest experienced record-breaking lows of snowfall over the season. In February I thought I'd try booking a mid-week stay again. I returned to Airbnb and reserved a 250-square-foot cottage nestled into someone's backyard on the edge of the Deschutes River about five minutes from downtown Bend.

Well, there was really no snow, so snowshoeing was out. I called some of the brewery bus tour services, but they were all booked even mid-week because of some master brewers' conference in town. The day I planned to drive out of Portland forecasted sideways rain/sleet, so the group hike I saw on Meetup was now cancelled. I wasn't going to cancel another Airbnb reservation, so I decided I'd road trip anyway.

I packed my laptop, a bottle of wine, various other essentials, and set off on the three hour drive east over Mt. Hood. There was no snow on the ground even at Government Camp. I stopped at the Warm Springs reservation Indian Head Casino to get lunch and gamble. I earned $25 playing Black Jack—enough to pay for my sandwich and a bit more.

I rolled into Bend a bit after 2 p.m. A gravel driveway took me past the host's house and to the picturesque cottage. The Airbnb ad did not lie—it was a beautiful open view of the river. It had a deck that led to wooden stairs, which brought one to the river's edge and a fully working hot tub. It was quiet and secluded. I resolved to make it a real writing retreat and spent the rest of the first day there churning out page after page on my laptop while I watched the rain pour into the river and whip against the large glass windows.

Still, I got antsy and wanted to branch out from my cottage. As it got dark that night, I drove out to the High Desert Museum to see a special exhibit on the history and ecology of craft brewing. For a small stipend, it was a thoroughly excellent two hours of my time spent reading about the usage of water from the Bull Run and the complicatedly beautiful process of hop growth to yield beer. And, as the Universe would have it, it happened to be tasting night! About five different breweries hosted tables with samples, and because it was February the theme of the month was porters vs. stouts—some of my favorite kinds of beer, especially in the winter. I garnered restaurant tips from the locals manning the beer stations and headed back into town to Brother Jon's Public House, where I ate dinner and drank more delicious pints. I took the leftovers back to my riverside retreat and slept soundly.[53]

I spent the whole next day writing, and after nightfall I carried my bottle of wine down to the hot tub when the rain stopped and the sky cleared. I soaked in the blissfully hot water under the white waning moon, listening to the river flow by, wondering at my luck that I would have the opportunity to indulge myself in such a way.

Have you stopped reading yet and started searching online for your next weekend getaway? Well, I'll go ahead and give you the opportunity right now. If you haven't already, download Airbnb (see Appendix A).

The whole place was amazing. I could hole myself up next to this river for the entire two-night stay and generate an eBook or two, but I wanted my solo road trip to pack more punch. Inspiration struck me right before leaving Portland, prompting me to hatch an absurd, nonsensical plan to cross No. 21 off my List, but I was going to need help.

No. 21
Enter a contest

Evening of February 6th, 2015 —

"What—is—that?" my friend Rashida exclaimed, looking in the back of my rental car. Her eyes popped upon seeing a

______

53   More about the High Desert Museum here: https://highdesertmuseum.org/

moderately-sized, green inflated donkey and a snowboard.

"That is a donkey," I replied. Rashida looked at me incredulously. "It's really a child's toy—you know one of those bouncy things for toddlers learning to walk? Oh, and that's a busted up snowboard."

"Uh huh. What are we going to do with them?" she asked.

Okay, I'll get to it, but first a little flashback.

Prior to leaving on my solo road trip I spent a good amount of time internet-searching things to do in the Bend area, since my original snowshoe/brew tour/hiking plan crumbled with the November snowstorm. That's when I discovered the beer exhibit at the High Desert Museum, a far better substitute to a brewery tour anyhow, and then an enticing opportunity at the neighboring resort town of Sunriver.

With a population less of than 1,400, Sunriver vacation homes sit within a net of hiking and biking trails, close to Mt. Bachelor's skiing and snowboarding. According to the all-knowing Internet, Sunriver's second annual Chill Out festival held varied events, including but not limited to a K-9 Keg Pull, guided nighttime snowshoeing with glow-in-the-dark lights, ice skating, and a Downhill Dummy Contest. This last event caught my eye. Participants were encouraged to create eccentric dummies secured to either skis or snowboards, and then push them down a hill of snow and over a ramp, hoping for aerodynamic glory and a spectacular crash landing. As I watched YouTube videos of last year's competition, I thought—YES! THAT'S IT! *Number 21!*

The organizers gave contestants size dimensions and weight restrictions, and encouraged a "family-friendly" nature. Too bad, otherwise I'd get a six-foot inflatable penis from a bachelorette party website and call it good. Alas, this was the challenge. A few days before leaving Portland for Bend I got on Craigslist and started searching for ideas based on previous entries, i.e. piñatas, stuffed animals, etc. I typed in "inflatable toys" into the Craigslist search engine.

Bad idea. Do not do this.

I typed in "inflated children's toy" —which brought me to the bouncy green donkey someone was giving away for $5. Score. Then I found the thrashed un-mountable snowboard for $15. I drove to get the snowboard first. I stuck the long blue thing in the back of my Jeep and set off to get the donkey…and then my engine wouldn't start.

Shit. Shit shit shit.

A few more expletives and prayers later I got my Jeep to run but I could tell she didn't have much longer. I kept the engine running as I picked up the amazingly perfect, bouncy green donkey and threw it in the back as well. Thankfully, an auto shop resided not more than a block away from the previous donkey owner's house.

Unfortunately, my beloved Jeep Liberty (affectionately named Ado Annie) had endured significant damage. She needed to be hospitalized for at least a week.

I was not going to cancel another reservation. I had already picked up two ridiculous items for a contest held three hours away. I booked a rental car and had an interesting time explaining to the auto shop workers and the rental car agency staff why I had to transfer a green donkey and a snowboard from my Jeep to a black Honda with limited storage. The looks they gave me varied from confused to careless. I said goodbye to Ado Annie, packed my rental, and headed to Bend.

Okay, fast forward.

I showed Rashida (celebrity casting: Rashida Jones) the donkey and snowboard sitting in the back of my rental car the night before the contest, about fifteen hours prior to the start time. I pulled up the YouTube video of last year's contest. She exclaimed, "Oh I'm in. We're so in. You know Seth is still at REI in the shop. He can wax the board for us."

Since my friendship with Rashida predates kindergarten, I bet correctly that she would be into the quirky project. Rashida and her husband Seth converted to Bendism[54] before they got married. We drove to REI where Rashida's husband Seth (celebrity casting: Seth Rogan) worked. I carried in the snowboard and handed it to Seth who looked at me suspiciously. I said, "I swear I'll explain later."

Seth had about an hour left working in the shop. Rashida and I hit up the Dollar Store to find accessories for the donkey. We took the donkey, the décor, and the snowboard back to Rashida and Seth's apartment after dinner. They offered a spot on their couch while I was in town, but I insisted on enjoying my Airbnb. I showed my dear friends the List, and showed the video to Seth—who absolutely freaked out. He took the snowboard downstairs to his tool table set up next to the fishing boat, snowshoes, and mountain gear (again, Bendism) and screwed wood into the base. He attached a box to the wood and filled it with weights. We then mounted the green donkey on the box and secured it with an embarrassing amount of duct tape. Rashida and I

---

54   Bendism: When Oregonians tire of Portland's maddening hipster-vegan/rainy/overcrowded/transient-infested city and vacate permanently to Central Oregon's paradise full of outdoor sporting, lack of traffic, mass quantities of solitude, sunshine, and endless amounts of craft beer. Seriously, it's endless.

attached glittery toy batons to its sides with tinsel for wings, amongst other bedazzling agents, i.e. a Seattle Seahawks face tattoo, sparkly garland, and fuzzy socks.

The craftiness that consumed me in No. 19 resurfaced. Seth put a helmet on the donkey and a Seahawks tattoo for good luck. As soon as the helmet was on the monster, Rashida and I had the same epiphany and yelled out simultaneously: "It's Crash Test Donkey!"

Crash Test Donkey became the glorious Entry #8 for the Sunriver Chill Out's second annual Downhill Dummy Contest 2015.[55] Because it was such a mild winter, the organizers of the event had snow delivered from higher ground down to the resort area. They erected a hill with a slope and a steep ramp. The ramp appeared much larger than the one in the video from the prior year. We examined the other entries and wished we had added more weights to the box attached to our snowboard. We also noted that our Donkey was the only contestant on a snowboard instead of fixed skis. The lineup was impressive; it included a gas dispenser on skis—an advertisement for the local gas station—a leaping cheetah, a characterized vacuum, and others. The 10 a.m. event was free and attracted a modest but enthusiastic crowd. One could purchase hot chocolate or a doughnut for under a dollar.

The first four entries didn't even make it over the ramp. Everyone became nervous at the thought no character would be eligible for the Best Crash award; but finally, the leaping cheetah sled weighing in at around 70 lbs. made it over the ramp. It ended up winning Longest Jump.

Finally, it came time for Crash Test Donkey to have a

----

55   If you look at no other photos on the website for this book, find this one. I don't think my description really does the masterpiece justice. mariemacmillan.com/rebootphotos

run. With a rope tied to its front, Rashida and I hauled the brilliantly constructed masterpiece to the top of the hill and prayed for aeronautical success. Rashida and Seth both took video on their phones. At Rashida's request, I humored our childhoods by yelling, "Cool Runnings!" as I launched Crash Test Donkey down the snowy stretch.

It wobbled. It wavered.

It veered right and left a bit off target—it didn't look like it was going to quite make it over. We collectively squealed, cringed, and bit our lips—and *wheeee!*—Crash Test Donkey prevailed! It sailed humbly over the obstacle, made the least possible amount of air, and landed soundly on its board. No crash, but it did sink over on its side, as if the Donkey was so ready to get off that box, saying, "Never doing that again!"

Rashida and I hugged and hollered. Seth retrieved the monster at the bottom of the hill. We almost cried laughing over the videos from both angles. We didn't win any awards, and yet, victory. I will forever treasure the ridiculousness of that contest and the fun we had preparing for it.

I loaded Crash Test Donkey in my rental car, said goodbye to my dear old friends, and took to the highway back to my familiar Portland home nestled in the Willamette Valley full of rain, hipsters, and need-to-pay-bills reality; the memories of the solo trip worth every quizzical look I got as I unloaded Crash Test Donkey from my rental car back into my repaired Jeep. The donkey and snowboard currently sit in my basement storage room, waiting patiently for next year's contest.[56]

56　Sunriver did not put on the contest the following year, but I still have Crash Test Donkey.

Side Story #7
The Triple J and the Classiest F-You Ever Written

Warning: This section is rated NFP: Not for Prudes. Quickly assess Grandma's level of cool. Has she fallen asleep? Okay, then read to yourself until she wakes up. Mom and Dad—do yourselves a favor and skip to Part 4.

So come March 2015, I was sort of dating around a bit. Okay, not a bit. I was seeing a few guys somewhat simultaneously. I found this so fun, so entertaining, and so good for my self-esteem (See Side Story #6) that I got away from my List for a while. Hey, girls just wanna have fun. Oh-ooooh girls just wanna have fu-uuhhhnn…thank you Cyndi Lauper, thank you.

For writing purposes, I've given these three gentlemen celebrity castings as follows: John Krasinski, Jake Gyllenhaal, and Jai Courtney. John, Jake, and Jai. Of course, these are fictionalized interpretations of the real deals, whose names all started with the same letter and sounded similar enough I occasionally got mixed up with which dude told me which story about his truck/welding hobby/latest tattoo idea.

At the end of Side Story #4, I said I was done with considering Tinder as a way of legitimately meeting guys. That was true, until I recognized John on it—also the swiping is addicting. ADDICTING.

John and I played in the same adult rec sports league and I thought for years he was super good-looking, but I never actually went up and talked to him. Well, this time

I decided to swing the bat and messaged him first on the infamous dating app. He recognized me right away too, and we met up for drinks not long after…and ended up making out in a parking lot. John, an auto mechanic, was obsessed with his truck. In sum total, we went on three dates in a span of three months. They were nice dates, don't get me wrong, but I never felt like he was super interested. Every time I received a text with a photo of the latest upgrade to his truck instead of an invite to hang out, I got the feeling he was unavailable—because he was dating his truck.

I mean really, only three dates in three months? I decided I must not be lighting up his radar after the *third time* I asked him out and he had to sleep, work on his truck, scratch his balls, or whatever. Too bad, I actually liked him. Nice guy, just totally clueless. Or not interested. Either way, if anything was unattractive to me now it was indecisiveness, or blatantly making it obvious I wasn't a priority.

I found Jake on Tinder as well, amidst all the additional swiping—he got through the Algorithm (see Fig. 1). Once John seemed MIA, Jake started messaging me. His profile picture showed him in his hard hat with an orange vest on a construction job. Talk about a classic fantasy. Jake asked me out pretty quickly after chatting through the app. He definitely appeared more interested than John. He was an electrician and enjoyed working on home improvement. I don't know what came over me this spring—a blue collar wave of single working men. El Niño? No, more like Los Muchachos. Jake and I had probably four or five dates in a month's time, and the sex was fabulous—never have I ever had that much, um, repetition. Then, one time, at his house, I felt the all-too-familiar wave of disinterest. We just returned to the living room from his terribly messy bedroom. We sat down on the couch and watched a little NBA All-Star game coverage. After a few high-flying dunks I said I was going to take off.

"Alright, cool, later," he stated immediately and matter-of-factly, as I sat on the couch, unmoving.

"Alright…" I replied, slightly unnerved. I gathered my purse and stood up. His eyes never wavered from the television. I moved slowly over to the front door adjacent to the living room, watching his stagnant stare and feeling somewhat confused. I paused.

"Okay, bye," I said, twisting the door knob loudly, purposefully attempting to get a reaction from the robot-like behavior. Jake took a swig from his beer and made a tiny acknowledgement with his free hand, but never looked away from the TV. Trying to unlock my staunchly raised eyebrow, I exited and walked to my car somewhat alarmed. I knew he wasn't that much of an NBA fan.

Driving through Burgerville on my way home, I thought about how weird that seemed, that he didn't walk me to his door like even the sluttiest of one-night-standers would. He just sat there and waited for me to leave. I mean don't get me wrong, I didn't want to be anyone's girlfriend, but I didn't want to feel like complete trash either.

This is the part where the conservative readership might exclaim what goes around comes around (Mom, I told you to skip to Part 4!). This is where insecure assholes might call me a slut. This is where I tell them all to go back to Page 111 and reread the opening quote for Part 3.

You guys, I drove through a fast food restaurant on the way home, not a church confessional.

More or less, the bizarre non-goodbye pretty much did it for me. He didn't call or text until two weeks later—a casual: "What's up?"—after 10 p.m. on a Friday. *Psh*, yeah no. I didn't reply. I'm not a hot dog bun. Moving on.

So, to sum up my male interactions over the last six months, it was full of mediums and lows and rock bottoms. We've covered utter heartbreak (Side Story #1), lack of interest (as above), immediate regret after initiating coitus (Tinder Distraction #2), ghosting (Side Story #6), zero common ground (Tinder Distraction #1), complete douchebaggery (Tinder Distraction #3/multiple Side Stories), and impossible-to-ignore age differences (Side Story #5).

However, the Ultimate Prick of the Year Award goes to celebrity casting Jai Courtney in this Side Story #7.

A Corner Bar regular, Jai and I had informal conversations here and there over the last year. He kept telling me how hot I was. I pushed it off as any smart girl would, though I did think he was pretty sexy. (I mean really, have you seen Jai Courtney in *A Good Day to Die Hard* with Bruce Willis? Hot damn.) Finally, one night, Jai made his move, and I thought—*hey what the hell, okay*. At this point John was still hit-and-miss and the spark with Jake had fizzled. Mostly I was bored, so I took Jai home and marveled at the fact that he wasn't overstating his skills. I thought he was all talk and no game—an inaccurate bet on my part.

He wasn't a jerk—at least, initially—and he was cool with nothing serious. I was ecstatic. Only one other time in my life, many years ago, have I experienced a 100% conflict-free, purely casual, physical relationship. By this time in my List journey my emotional gas tank was still pointing toward Empty, so I was thrilled this was working out in my favor.

No awkwardness, pure honesty, zero drama; just good, clean, carnal fun. Securing a true Friend-with-Benefits with no ulterior motive is like finding a winged-unicorn hauling the Ark of the Covenant.

But, in the end, I don't want to associate myself with complete assholes—no matter how much of a tiger he might be in the sack. I don't care if his dick is 14 inches long and he delivers the Holy Grail of orgasms. Sometimes you need to run the hell away from unicorns. There is a reason they are mystically extinct.

One quiet night at the Corner Bar I waved to Jai before realizing he had a girl with him. *Oops*, I thought—no big deal though. It didn't bother me, I just wanted to say hi since I hadn't seen him in a few weeks. That was it, I honestly didn't think more of it.

Unfortunately, though, Jai decided to address an apparent rift between us I didn't know or care existed. Behold, verbatim excerpt (seriously, copied-and-pasted) from Jai Courtney's less-than-innocuous exit from my life, via private Facebook message:

For the past few months, I've been going through a really hard time emotionally. Things with me and my ex weren't completely over. At least in my mind and heart. Come to find out she met someone and planned a trip to Hawaii with him. That stung a bit. Actually a lot. Still hurts. I'm struggling a lot right now mentally. I've started seeing a counselor. I need to get me right again. As far as you and I, I haven't made an attempt because there was something that turned me off. I need to be honest with you. Please in no way take what I'm about to say negative. It's more to inform you. I think you are absolutely gorgeous. You have one of the most amazing bodies I've ever seen. We connected in the bedroom, as well as in normal life. The last time we were together, I noticed you had quite a bit of hair on your nipples. I know it happens and most girls get it, but to me that's a huge turn off. I like a woman who takes care of themselves hygienically. Not saying you don't, but scaping certain areas where there shouldn't be hair, is a must for me. I do it for the ladies, I'd hope they'd do it for me. What I like.....

> *Shaved legs, unless last minute. Understandable.*
> *Shaved armpits*
> *Shaved or trimmed and clean vagina*
> *No excessive hair in general areas.*
> *No nipple hair*
> *No mustache*
> *Clean eyebrows*
> *No butt crack hair*

If this makes me shallow, then so be it. I understand something's are more important than others, but it's just the way I feel. I want to have sexual relations with someone who takes care of themselves in all aspects. I'd think a woman would want the same of me. So, I apologize if I'm being to forward. If I can't be honest, what can I be? Just like not telling someone they have bad breath. They can't fix the issue if no one will stand up and just tell them. And if they don't consider it an issue, so be it. I hope you can understand what I'm saying. If you hate me after this, I totally understand. Again, in no way am I not attracted to you. There was just that turn off that got me. I'm sorry. I hope you have a wonderful day. Hope you're not mad at me. Just trying to be real and open. Maybe talk soon. -Jai

What I typed in reply:

FUCK OFF you piece of shit asshole. I really didn't care whether we continued to sleep together or not. Seriously. Did you think you were doing me a favor by pointing out supposedly unappealing parts of my body? Well I love my body so you can go suck your own dick. I mean who the hell do you think you are, Dr. Phil? Did you think I thought every inch of you was wonderfully perfect? I'll be sure to mail you an itemized list of areas needing improvement. You are the shallowest prick I've ever come across. You obviously have no idea what women want, you miserable asshat. Good luck finding your perfect blow-up teenage sex doll, I'm sure Craigslist can help you get started. Or maybe your therapist can come up with a healthy solution, like maybe a combination of Prozac, Viagra, Vaseline and an HBO subscription. Don't talk to me or my perfectly beautiful hairy nipples ever again YOU FUCKING CALLOUS DOUCHEBAG.

Okay, I erased it before hitting Send. Here's what I wrote instead, after an hour of fuming and deleting variations of the above:

Jai - sorry to hear about your emotional struggle, hope you are able to work that out. As far as the rest of your message, honestly a simple "You're great but I'm just not into it anymore" would have been sufficient. We weren't ever exclusive on any level so you don't owe me any other explanation. I really did not need an itemized list of your personal feelings about my body in critique form. I welcome honesty about where a relationship is headed or not headed, but your other comments could have been left unsaid and unwritten. It was overkill, unnecessary, and altogether not classy. Typically, I don't provide partners with a list of what's not sexy about them, and in attempts at being cordial and mature I'll continue that trend and not provide you with one. Honestly, I just wanted to say hi the other night and catch up. So no I don't hate you, but no I don't like you anymore and we won't be friends. So other than that good luck with your endeavors.

As a young, malleable Catholic, I was taught I'd never regret taking the higher ground. I'm not convinced about that on this one. I really really wanted to send my first message. Alas, my mother's Golden Rule reiterations won out in the end. And to you critics out there knitting a big red letter A, just stop. I'm not a slut, I'm selectively promiscuous; and if that makes me "dirty" well then, I'm going to be the classiest, most-polite, admittedly-sexual woman around. You're welcome.

Not sure what I should call this "opposite of ghosting phenomenon" where the guy graphically describes why he's just not that into you…Unfiltered honesty? Hmm, doesn't have a ring to it. While I don't want to be strung along I also don't want my shortcomings, physical or otherwise, illustrated on a vividly unambiguous level in written form no less for ease of referral.

Dim-witted Possessor of Forgettable Dick? Testicles attached to Brainless Man? Miserably Tactless Asshole? Ugh, I'll need to work on this. I really do like the last line of my original un-sent message: Fucking Callous Douchebag.

So, the Triple J was no more. John and I remained friends and said hi to each other once in awhile. He and his truck are reportedly very happy together. I never heard from Jake again. And as for Jai—I can't say I didn't giggle with delight when I heard through the Corner Bar grapevine that he got indefinitely 86'd a few months later for calling another female patron a "Bitch, slut, and whore!" to her face. Talk about having issues. Remember that Karma thing I was talking about before?

The single-people cesspool had me exhausted and bewildered yet again. Unicorns, and Tinder, and Facebook—

oh my. I was gathering quite the spectrum of interludes, from the predictably mediocre to the romantically catastrophic. Though I regret nothing, because I get to live this life and tell you fine folks about it.

Hey, Grandma, wake up, the story's not over yet—just a handful of Dates left to go.

Part 4

The last ten Dates

Don't ever give up
Your day will definitely come
You can feel it too, can't you?
Your first beat

— Anonymous pedestrian tunnel graffiti/poetry, near
McLoughlin Promenade in Oregon City,
see No. 24

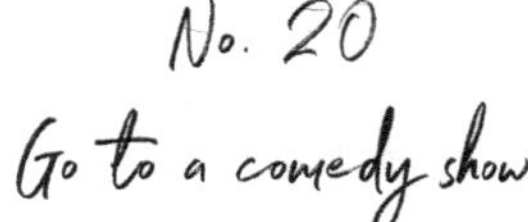

February 27th, 2015—Who doesn't love a good laugh, right? I bought a solitary ticket to a premier performance at Helium Comedy Club—the leading jokester showcase in the city. I just picked the next show that fit in my variable hospital shift life.

What can I say; Taylor Williamson headlined a pretty funny shindig. I sat at a table by myself and definitely met the two-drink minimum. I laughed. I didn't garner much inspiration for No. 16, but I had a decent time. I was beginning to feel more comfortable going stag to couple-y things. I was beginning to care less about how I might appear to other people, and I became infatuated with my ability to have a fantastic time alone—self-love at its finest, no joke about it.

No. 49
Volunteer for kids somewhere doing something productive

March 10th, 2015 — With my fickle schedule I found it pretty difficult to lock down a volunteer opportunity. Weird, right? Well, turns out most organizations that work with kids want a solid weekly commitment of a few hours, regularly and/or indefinitely, and with that comes pretty thorough background screenings. Not that I have anything to hide, I just didn't feel the need to get a bunch of personal and professional recommendations from peers for a one-time thing. I had real interest in Boys and Girls Club, or Girls Inc., or Campfire, but they needed similar commitments. I looked at the children's hospital for volunteering, same thing. I didn't want to involve myself in special needs children, or do one-on-one tutoring. I had to dig to find something that fit. Ideally, I imagined myself playing soccer with a bunch of elementary school kids. There I could thrive, or teaching health. Honest to God, I'd quit my nursing job and teach high school health and sex-ed tomorrow if it paid as well.

However, I found a volunteer-matching organization called Hands On Portland. Their calendar listed all sorts of one-day-only opportunities. I found a need for volunteers for a city-sponsored one-day teaching program called the Clean Water Festival. According to its webpage, it provides environmental education for fourth and fifth graders in a one-day extravaganza by reinforcing, "STEM, Common Core and Next Generation Science concepts through water-focused classroom presentations, exhibits and stage shows," on a local university campus. I volunteered to be a class guide.

I arrived at the ass crack of dawn, *ahem,* sorry the crack of dawn (need watch my language around the minors). I picked up a green volunteer vest, a schedule, a map of the college campus, free coffee and breakfast. I got to be in charge of getting twenty-five fourth graders, their teacher, and chaperones from point A to point B throughout the day. Sessions lasted about twenty-five minutes each and allowed about ten minutes in-between to walk, take bathroom breaks, etc.

At 8:05 a.m. I had my vest on, my clipboard, my smallest REI backpack, and a smile, waiting for the bus labeled [Forgettable School District Name]. Once said bus arrived, I hopped on board, introduced myself as their Super Awesome Class Guide for the day, shouting: "Who's ready to learn about water?!" and the kids shouted back, "MEEEE!!!!"

Oh my God, it was so much fun. I should have been a camp counselor. Fourth graders are the best. They haven't hit puberty yet so they still think boys/girls are gross/gross and generally separate according to gender; but they aren't snarky or whiny at all, and they listen to directions. When we had to walk outside between classroom buildings, we played one or two running games like Red Rover. When it was time to move on, I had them all gather in, put their hands in the center of the group, and shout their mascot. *Go Mascots!*

I got a lot of questions about my age. I told them it was fourteen times two, which took them a minute to figure out, and by then they likely forgot and became wrapped up in their buddy's discussion about the latest video game or

Taylor Swift song—again, boys and girls. Some of them came back to me with the exclamation, "Twenty-eight! Whoa!!!!!" Like it was number they would never be able to reach ever in their lives, like beating their Xbox game or getting to actually talk to Taylor Swift. I suppose many ten-year-olds don't get exposure to twentysomethings. We're like mystical creatures to them. What do they eat? Where do they live? Who do they live with? What do they wear? Do they sit in a tree, k-i-s-s-i-n-g? It's a mystery.

I led the lively group to a cafeteria where everyone ate. Volunteers were provided box lunches. After a breezy twenty-minute gobbling session I gathered them up (lots of head counting) and marched them to the last show: a solo circus performer's interpretation of the science of water preservation. Literally, the guy balanced himself on a big ball and juggled low-flow efficiency shower heads to make his point. The kids loved it.

I walked the group back to their bus before 1 p.m. and waved goodbye. Their teacher told me I should do things like this more, and that I do well with kids. I agreed with her, about fourth graders anyway. Not sure I'd want to handle whimpering first graders or texting teenagers.

I'm pretty proud to live in a place where publicly funded money goes to educational programs geared toward science and environmentally conscious living. Knowledge is power and kids are hope.

If you are on a journey to better yourself, I highly suggest finding an activity that works with kids. It's a good reminder of what it was like to be one and that we all have a responsibility to leave the world a better place for them. Not to mention, it's a cue to admit that your own personal sob story is miniscule compared to the challenges of climate change, public education, and the future of humanity on this planet.

No. 45
Do something scary, scarier than your normal every day scary.

By every day scary I meant my work life full of biohazards, heart monitors, difficult truths, medical responsibility and body bags. Certainly, many of the already completed Dates could considerably satisfy this requirement, for example No. 29, No. 48, and No. 12. However, I was explicitly following my intention to not overlap or double count Dates. Insert Bruce Willis's voice, a là the movie *Armageddon*: I will make 50 Dates. I swear to God I will.

Interestingly, the List of 50 Dates inspired me to bravely do other things not even related to things on the List. In January, I booked a weeklong vacation in Florida. Granted, I had a funeral to attend and friends there to visit, but I could have done that in a weekend. I chose to stay a whole week and got a few base tan layers going after the initial sunburn while finishing a few novels just feet from the Atlantic Ocean.

I hosted Easter Sunday Brunch and cooked for twelve family members.

I went roller skating for the first time since someone's tenth birthday party.

Later, in June, I successfully and truly conquered my fear of riding a bike (see Side Story #9).

I continued to go out on dates with boys because I wasn't giving up on love. I embodied a "don't say no" attitude. If someone invited me to go somewhere or try something new, I made it happen. If I saw something on a blog or in *Willamette Week* that looked entertaining, I tried to make it happen. I wasn't saying no to fun, the possibility of fun, or crazy lively experiences just because they were expensive, or outlandish, or scary.

On the one hand, letting yourself go in this manner isn't necessarily brave at all. Like when Emma called me to ask if I wanted to accompany her to Napa Valley to wine taste for three straight days, "under $300, whenever it fits in your schedule, I'll do all the planning, just come with me," — yeah, that shit isn't difficult to say no to. *Have as much fun as possible*—doesn't sound tough, right? A wonderful excursion to California led to an excessively lascivious birthday weekend for Emma and me in Las Vegas in May—which could fill a whole separate book entitled "Side Story #NeverAgain," but what happened there stays there.

(Okay fine, here's a hint: Vegas + Side Story #6 + A Bachelor Party + plenty of Tinder Fail #3s = new meaning to the phrase "hair of the dog." Use your imagination.)

Anyway, my point is that sometimes the scariest things in life happen to be things just needing to get done, you know the *not fun* things—the anti-Vegas things. For me, that happens to circle right around doing the dishes, visits to my gynecologist, and financial matters. The world won't end if I wash my dinnerware according to the easy, stress-free process described by author Kelly Williams Brown (see Appendix A), but why risk it? And as far as my gynecologist goes…I think the ringtone I have saved for her office is Bob

Marley's reassuring *Everything's Gonna Be Alright*. Nice lady my doctor, don't get me wrong, I just wish she didn't show up under "frequent contacts."

And money? Ugh. I'd rather walk barefoot through the Corner Bar parking lot full of broken glass, cigarette butts, and unidentifiable fluids than sift through the details of my retirement savings. My head hurts at the mention of phrases like W2, 403B, IRA, and—*gulp*—investments. I get heart palpitations trying to collect my tax receipts. Although, my dad has taught me well in the ways of avoiding financial stupidity—I was trained to never accrue credit card debt and to pay off any interest I amassed—but I purposefully avoid the finer nuances of gaining economic intelligence. It makes my brain hurt. I will probably wash all my dishes and rearrange the contents of my kitchen cabinets or schedule my next Pap smear before analyzing my credit card spending.

But a giant bank-related victory got me to face the scary money monster. As of this February, I became college debt free (*Woooooo! Millennial win!!!*) and decided I could breathe and not worry about money, just pay my rent and bills and have fun.

Alas, my dear old paid-off Jeep Liberty had other plans. Her stay at the auto-hospital proved painful to not only her but my checking account. I realized after a bit of research that if I bought a new car it would save me money, for all the repair cash I was throwing at old Ado Annie. Much as I loved her, much as I held the memories of the last ten years close to me, it was time to put her out to pasture.

I downloaded several advice books and spent an inordinate amount of time perusing the Kelley Blue Book. I read several "How to Not Fuck Up Buying a Car" tip sheets and a commendably invaluable guide by Beth Kobliner entitled *Get a Financial Life* (see No. 17). Again, don't get me wrong, I'm not financially stupid—but I could be financially smarter. This will end up being the largest purchase I've made in my life to date, and I know those sharks at the auto dealers will nickel and dime an unmarried white girl like me with a credit score above 800.

I wanted to be ultra-prepared. I wanted to make sure I brought my heavy-duty tranquilizer gun with me in the ocean of parked cars where sales Sharks could pop their ugly fins up at any moment. After all, I worked hard for my income, to pay off my education, and I wasn't going to let a greasy motherfucker with a commission incentive get the best of me and my checking account.

March 19th, 2015—The day arrived. I had already done methodical research. John from Side Story #7 was actually really helpful—talking about cars was the only way I could get him to text me back ever. I had test driven six models at four different dealerships. What can I say, I was the atypical car shopper. I was told the likelihood of a prospective new car owner returning to a dealership after leaving without a new vehicle is nearly zero; which explains why they try really really really hard to not let you leave. They throw all sorts of deals and discounts at you. But I was determined. I wanted to find the best car for the best price.

In my best jeans, heels, and a nice purple blouse that showed just the right amount of boob, I arrived at Dealer #1 of 3 around noon. I stepped out of Ado Annie, armed with my printed credit report and preapproved loan confirmations, and walked straight up to the Sharks in suits waiting at the entrance, practically licking their lips at the thought of my bank accounts. The *Jaws* theme played in my head. I took off my sunglasses, did a little hair swish, holstered my tranquilizer gun and asked:

"Who wants to show me a five-seat SUV with all-wheel drive under twenty-five thousand?"

I was a fucking Superbowl commercial. I was terrified, but I was ready.

Dealer #1 did well; I liked the model. I liked the people. I was near getting sucked under to purchase, but I held on. I straight up told them my strategy: I was going to test drive my top three choices and pick by the end of the day. I was going to leave their dealership no matter what.

They didn't like that. The first Shark passed me off to the next level up Shark, who ended up passing me to the Managing Shark—they were showing me their best game. Managing Shark told me to write down a price number I was okay with. I wrote down $100. Managing Shark laughed, but good-naturedly. He went behind his desk, printed out some numbers, and came back to where Shark Levels 1 and 2 were attempting to woo me at one of their fancy tables. He said: "I've been doing this a long time. I can tell you have a plan and won't budge, so I'll let you carry it out. Here's my best deal. You call me before the end of the day." He handed me his card.

Dealer #2 was a total shit show. Sharks making wild statements left and right, I could see the other customers' limbs flying and blood splattering across the dealership floor. Their Managing Shark told me not to run my credit score at any other dealers, it would ruin my financing. I shot off a few tranquilizers and left shortly after the test drive. I didn't like their model any better anyhow.

Dealer #3 showed promise. A Kid Shark who took me out driving just the day before made a real case. We took a super long test drive. I think he was flirting with me, and not just for my money. Kid Shark played the same game as all the other Sharks though, asked me what he could do to make me drive away in one of their vehicles. I told him I was going to take his best offer and go mull it over a chocolate milkshake and call him back. Kid Shark's boss, Other Managing Shark, came out to me sitting at one of their plain tables. He asked the same question, I gave the same answer. Kid Shark made an awkward attempt at trying to invade my milkshake party by offering to drive me to the burger joint in the prospective new car and buy me the milkshake himself. At that point I had to zip a dart into him too. Poor Kid Shark.

Slurping a tall delicious chocolate milkshake, I looked at my two really good deals and went with my gut. Kid Shark did a good job, but I ended up back at Dealer #1 writing Managing Shark a hefty check. He took $5,000 off the list price and gave me 0% interest on my five-year loan. Level 1 and Level 2 Sharks tried to sell me bells and whistles, which I politely declined. A Level 3 Shark had me go through the hardcore paperwork and finishing touches of the sell. After a few signatures and some yawns he said to me, "You know, I saw you all over these dealerships yesterday and today, and you were smiling the whole time. I'm gonna give you an extra discount on [bells and whistles offered by Levels 1 and 2 Sharks]." At that point I accepted, with a smirk. Levels 1 and 2 Sharks were super pissed when they heard. Once I realized I held the power, it became fun.

I gave Ado Annie one last goodbye pat before trading

her in. A quick flash of ten years and 300,000 miles flickered through my mind. I left the dealership at 9 p.m. in my shiny new 2015 Toyota RAV4. Black exterior, black interior. The first song that blared through her speakers: Beyoncé's *Drunken Love*—for which she was christened Black Beauty.

No. 4
Participate in a hiking group

April 19th, 2015—I tried and tried and tried and tried to get this one organized. It seems stupid, seeing as I live in the Pacific Northwest and hiking season is long and bountiful. I tried through Meetup, a group activity app, but could never find a good time and location that fit my schedule. Many of those Meetup hikes were for special group members only, or were at night, or were for long distances. I didn't want to pay a stipend to go hike a trail with strangers when I could do it for free with friends. I didn't want to hike in the city. I didn't go hiking to see urban landscape, I wanted mountains damnit. I didn't want to hike at night and I didn't want to sign up for something over ten miles with people I never met before. What if they all simply sucked at being people and I wanted to tear my eyeballs out after Mile 3? What if the leader didn't know what he or she was doing on the ledge of a difficult trail? Not a situation I desired to find myself in.

April rolled around and I had to bust this one out, even if it wasn't in the way I imagined it—with lots of cool, young hiking enthusiasts for two or three hours during the daytime outside city limits.

My old friends Rashida and Seth happened to be in town

to celebrate Rashida's dad's 60th birthday party. Rashida's dad Michael (celebrity casting: Michael Keaton) was an avid hiker, mountain climber, and outdoorsman. He instructed climbing classes for the Mazamas, a 121-year-old Portland-area mountaineering organization. I got a text from Rashida that they were going hiking and invited me along. I thought okay, this will count. I basically had a professional guide, it was daytime, it was way outside the city, and I got to see mountains.

We met at Michael's house and drove a few hours east to Catherine Creek Trailhead on the Washington side of the Columbia River. Michael has known me since I was in diapers. Rashida and I met at a toddler playtime group while our mothers sat next to each other pregnant with our younger sisters.

The three-mile loop and 500-foot gain was easy and steady and gave us plenty of time to catch up. Michael inquired about Dufus, so I had to catch him up on that. He sympathized generously, and told me I should learn climbing and date a climber. I told him I'd think about it. Honestly though, Michael is a wonderful man who I wholeheartedly admire—a proud father, grandfather, and single man at sixty living life every day as if it was his last. He joked that he just didn't tell his life insurance company about it, or about his gravity-defying mountaineering and ice-climbing habits.

Rashida brought her super high-tech camera and got as many closeup wildflower shots as possible. We ate our packed lunch at the top, looking at a brilliant view of the northeast rim of Mount Hood. We trekked back down carefully, and passed several large hiking groups and birdwatching clusters. As a foursome we bypassed them easily, Seth commenting on their ostentatious presence and lack of concern for the trail. To these Bendism converts, the big groups represented clueless tourists—you know, the ones who step off a huge bus, take photos with their cameras, dump their trash, and get back on the bus. Maybe hiking groups were overrated. I had a lovely time with my old friends and thanked the Universe for letting me miss out on the pretentious group hikes I had been internet-searching before.

The next night, I met up with Rashida and Seth, Rashida's sister Anna (Faris), and about fifty-plus other friends of Michael's at a pub. He was elated and surprised at the party. Anna made a cake iced in the image of a glacier with a tiny Michael climber figure set on it. They showed a slideshow of photos from his captivating sixty years—when his girls were little, when he led climbing expeditions, when he graduated college, with Anna's two kids, etc. One can only hope to attain his level of fulfillment at any point in life. I could see the enlightenment Michael achieved by simply being outdoors. He told me to check out Young Mazamas. I pledged to get outdoors as much as possible that summer, and maybe try climbing.

May 1st, 2015—I love Opening Night. The air of excited frenzy, the palpable tension, the tangible anticipation—I can't resist any of it. I love theatre. Perhaps this is why this was No. 1 because it was the first thing I thought of when I initially asked myself the question: "Where do you want to take yourself out on a Date?"

Every Opening Night I attend I try to imagine what the playwright might feel at a world premiere. On this occasion, I snagged a hot ticket to the resident opening of *Grounded*, a recently produced new play by George Brant, staged this April at the Public Theater in New York, starring Anne Hathaway and directed by Julie Taymor. Locally, Coho Productions' 99-seat black box theater came alive with a near-packed house awaiting the one-woman show starring Rebecca Lingafelter and directed by Isaac Lamb.

A *New York Times'* review of the play surmises: "Mr. Brant's play draws a nuanced and haunting portrait of a woman serving in the United States Armed Forces coming under pressure as the human cost of war, for combatants as well as civilians, slowly eats away at her well-armored psyche."

Lingafelter sold it. It's so difficult to keep an audience engaged with a plain set and one character. Lingafelter's pilot verbally conveyed military action and drone control from a solitary chair, imperceptibly thousands of miles away from her targets. While some parts were tough to chew, I appreciated the overall message—what kind of people are we turning into if we can't actually see the enemies we're striking down? One of many questions I have for Hillary Clinton, right after who makes her sunglasses and has she copyrighted her facial expressions yet.

After the metaphorical curtain, I walked to a nearby fancy-shmancy French restaurant to have a cocktail and a few munchies, to celebrate the night. If I close my eyes, I can still feel the nauseating pressure of performing from my youth. My twenty-eight-year-old self found it absolutely wonderful to just be an audience member, and dreamt that maybe someday I'll have the distinguished time-honored pleasure of having my stage work categorically torn apart by a reputable media outlet.

No. 31

Take an art class, or finish an art project already in process. Spend at least half a day on it.

May 3rd, 2015—Okay, so I'm a craft nut. I'm a fan of glue guns and shiny objects. I've tried my hand at painting, and have had little success. There are only two canvases hanging in my apartment and about eight tucked away in my sunroom never to see a wall mount again. This project entailed a multimedia paper collage glued on canvas.

Alright, so I didn't spend one half-day on it. This was a few years in the making. It started with one canvas frame, which I constructed in my first downtown apartment years ago, inspired by my initial downtown experiences living in the Southwest Goose Hollow neighborhood. Then Northwest Portland became the second muse, followed by Southeast, which is the sum of what I had accomplished prior to writing the List. Three collaged canvases hung on my walls in different rooms representing three of the five "quadrants" of Portland. I had two in the five-part series left to create. I wrote No. 31 with the completion of this particular project in mind.

It took me about a week or so to map my already-cut out and divided paper imagery, stashed away in a shoe box labelled NE and N. I took one trip to the craft store for matte finish paper glue. The project overran my living room; my artwork table in the sunroom wasn't large enough for it. After two weeks and ruining one pair of old jeans, I finished the five-part series depicting Portland's five quadrants and my overall adoration for my hometown. On May 3rd I hung the five canvases in my bedroom, next to each other in no particular order, hanging at different heights.

I love that this polyptych is one of the first things I see when I wake up in the morning.

No. 17
Spend an afternoon drinking wine reading a novel.

I lost count how many times I did No. 17.

Here is all the literature I read (or reread) while drinking wine, or not, since beginning my List journey:

- *30 First Dates*, a novel by Stacey Wiedower, 2015
- *Adulting: How to Become a Grownup in 468 Easy(ish) Steps*, a nonfiction masterpiece by Kelly Williams Brown, 2013
- *Being Mortal*, nonfiction look at end-of-life culture by Atul Gawande
- *Get a Financial Life: Personal finance in your twenties and thirties*, a valuable guidebook by Beth Kobliner, 2009
- *Inherit the Wind*, a play—my favorite play ever—by Jerome Lawrence and Robert E. Lee, 1955
- *It's Called a Break-up Because It's Broken: The Smart Girl's Break-up Buddy*, a nonfiction self-help chronicle by Greg Behrendt and Amiira Ruotola-Behrendt, 2006
- *Desire Under the Elms*, a play by Eugene O'Neill, 1924
- *The Help*, a novel by Kathryn Stockett, 2009

- *One Last Blind Date*, a novel by Erin Brady, 2014
- *The Sea-Gull*, a comedy in four acts, Anton Chekov, 1896
- *Sex with Strangers*, a play by Laura Eason, 2009
- *The Single Woman's Sassy Survival Guide*, a nonfiction self-help book by Mandy Hale, 2012
- *Wild*, a memoir by Cheryl Strayed, 2012
- *You Suck at Drinking*, the funniest/truest thing I've ever read about drinking, by Matthew Latkiewicz, 2015
- Please see Appendix A for recommendations.

Side Story #8
The Pen Pal Effect

So, I ditched Tinder. Really this time—but, I did decide to try a different online dating app called Hinge. It had more potential, but was based on the same working protocol—the swiping remained but the pool of applicants was reduced to people you had friends in common with on social media. I thought this concept of social proximity might bear more fruitful romance than the blind hookup approach. Worth a swing anyway.

I didn't have as many matches with this app, but the bachelors seemed to be superior in quality with mostly improved correct spelling capability. I matched with one guy—let's call him Jason (celebrity casting Jason Segel)—and we kind of hit it off. We chatted often through the app, which eventually gave way to me breaking my rule of not dishing my phone number to strangers. He never asked how horny I was, what I was wearing, or whether I'd be down for a threesome. He asked where I went to school, where I'd like to travel to, what sports teams I cheered for.

Jason had my attention, but I was growing wary of his reluctance to make solid plans to meet. It was always, "This week isn't good with work—but I definitely want to meet you, let's shoot for this Friday," and then something came up Friday, but the vibe remained flirtatious and interested. One time, we were even at the same Timbers match and failed to make a face-to-face connection. Okay, twenty-two thousand other people were at the game too, but still, he had little valid excuse for not making the effort, right? Sigh. My patience waned.

I was going to give Jason one more chance to meet. It was now twenty-eight days since we first messaged each other, more than enough time to squeeze in a one-hour coffee or beer meetup, or whatever, something. I gave this guy entirely too much leverage—but he seemed endlessly classier than anyone else I encountered online. We finally agreed on after work drinks.

The day of I had a long work meeting for one of the hospital committees I chaired. I desperately needed a haircut and what better time to get that taken care of than on the eve of a blind date? My hairstylist sucked out of me that I had a first date planned. She offered to style my hair a little sexier than average and curled it after hacking off two inches. I bedazzled my face with a moderate amount of makeup to highlight. I left the salon after a quick "Before and After" glamour shot and Instagram posting for her hairstylist account, and then headed to my meeting wearing jeans, a blouse, ankle boots, and nice earrings. You know, looking hot but not like I was trying all that hard, like I effortlessly looked amazing all the freaking time.

My committee adjourned early around 4 p.m. and I hadn't received any messages from Jason yet. I was waiting to hear from him after his work day ended to agree on a location, so I wandered over to Mississippi Street for happy hour to down a glass of wine and calm my nerves.

My leniency ended right around 6:30 p.m. when I had yet to receive a text or call. Instead of spending one more solitary minute of my precious time wondering, I texted him. I asked if he was still interested in meeting that night. The reply hovered around a "legitimate work emergency" that kept him questionably stranded until…nah fuck that! I call bullshit. It has been twenty-eight days! Even if tonight's excuse was justifiable, I wasn't waiting around anymore.

I was so miserably done writing and reading conversations sent over cyberspace that weren't actually going to evolve into face-to-face rhetoric. I was no longer going to give men the privilege of spending time with me if I didn't feel like a priority in their lives—and I was done doing the chasing, because I'm way better than that. I am worth being chased. Let me type that again for emphasis.

I am worth being chased.

Here's the text conversation with Jason Segal:

Me: Hey are you still interested in meeting tonight?

Jason: Hey yeah so sorry I can't tonight [insert questionably legitimate excuse/definite bullshit]…

Me: Well Jason, that's just too bad. I'm sorry to say I am not in the market for a pen pal and I have to move on. Good luck.

Jason: Lol okay?

I shook my head and slapped my palm to my forehead.

I guess I wasn't technically stood up, since the plans of where and when were never solidified, but it felt like it. I signed the bill at my table for one and took to walking the historic Mississippi Street in North Portland. Once again, my online dating hopes were dashed. Ah well, I had enough entertaining stories of amorous blunders over the last nine months I didn't need more. In fact, I deleted Hinge right then and there. I deleted whatever apps took up memory on my phone that even mimicked online courtship. I said to myself—*Fuck dating. I need a sabbatical. I'm officially on a guy-atus.*

I looked at the time—6:52 p.m. I began furiously searching on my phone for another option to entertain myself that lovely early summer evening. After all, I looked super nice with my salon hair and didn't feel like wasting the night pouting about a stupid boy who couldn't carve time out of his month-long schedule for a hot girl with a badass sense of humor and disposable income. I mean, sounds like someone I'd like to take out—but whatever, his loss.

I had only three Dates left to cross off: No. 25 (Go on a walking tour somewhere), No. 16 (Try open mic night)—and of course, the celebratory No. 50.

Still done up and first-date-impression-worthy, I moved to get one of the first two crossed off that night. I got back in my car and headed Southeast. The all-knowing internet informed me of a last-minute open mic night at a coffee shop. I arrived a tad early amongst many people with guitars congregating around the entrance, warming up their Joplin-esque voices with original songs. I walked inside, where people gathered on soft pillows surrounding a tiny open area, but no mic. I walked up to the coffee counter and asked the barista about the event. He slid the sign-up sheet over toward me.

"Oh, thanks, um, is there no microphone?" I asked him.

"Nope," he replied.

"Oh, okay. Does everyone sing with guitars?"

"Yeah pretty much."

"Oh, okay. Do you have a keyboard here?"

"Let me check in back," he said disappearing for a moment. "No, we don't, sorry."

"Okay, well…" I felt bad for even coming into the coffee shop. I didn't want to sing acapella in front of a bunch of hippies high on more than their music. That's just sad.

"Can I get an iced green tea latte?" I asked, pulling out my wallet. Maybe I'd stay and listen.

"Sure, what kind of milk?" Barista Man queried.

"What options do I have?"

"Half, whole, skim, soy, almond, cashew, coconut, or goat," he reeled off, "all organic."

"Surprise me," I replied, unable to process the selections or prevent myself from rolling my eyes. The result was a light green latte over ice in a compostable to-go cup. I picked up the latte, looked around at the pillow dwellers, and decided to get the hell out of there. Just…just not my scene right now. I was wearing heels and looked like I just got stood up—and that I obviously cared more about my hygiene than anyone else in the building.

I walked out. I headed to a parked Black Beauty. I took a sip of my latte, and gagged. It was disgusting. A total waste of $6.50. I dumped the contents into the next front yard I came across—angry that this was how my night was going— and tossed the biodegradable cup in the nearest municipal compost bin where it would probably take a long time to actually biodegrade. A neat metaphor for the beginning of the evening and my first swing at open mic night.

Alas, I was not that easily defeated. Unwilling to postmark the evening so soon without any adventure, I started up Black Beauty and headed south on Highway 99. Amazing what perseverance the right hairspray can give you.

No. 25
Go on a walking tour somewhere

Evening of June 11th, 2015—I found myself cruising all the way to Oregon City, still somewhat unable to get the taste of the green tea latte foible out of my mouth.

During all of my many automobile test drives (I think I did nine total, because I'm weird and over-plan when something terrifies me) I took routes through downtown Oregon City. The town historically competed with Portland for business and attention in the 19th century, but now had that quaint small-town charm. I distinctly remembered passing a prominent telescope-like landmark several times in different small SUVs, thinking—*Huh, that's cool, what is that?*

In 1915, all three-thousand residents of Oregon City rode a newly constructed hydraulic elevator that took one from the level of the Willamette River up to the top of the bluff, bypassing the 700 old earthen steps. Ten years later, hydraulic power was replaced by electricity and by 1955 a newer model supplanted the original. Today, the elevator remains a historic yet also functional crowning piece of the town and brags one of the best views of the Willamette

River, also maintaining the tradition of free rides in true municipal fashion. Apparently, Elevator Street is the only "vertical" street in North America.

I parked Black Beauty in downtown Oregon City, and walked down the hallway that dipped under the railroad tracks. The hallway led to the elevator doors. It took only fifteen seconds to ride to the top, during which I endured uncomfortable staring from the elevator attendant. However, the view from the top was pretty spectacular. The holographic historical placards were fun as well. I wandered for about fifteen minutes before the creepy elevator attendant asked if I was enjoying myself. I cringed, smiled politely, and nodded my head. He then informed me about a trail that went from the top of the Elevator down the bluff to Willamette Falls. I thanked him for the tip and walked down the trail in the waning sunshine, my stiffly curled hair blowing in the warm wind.

It was nice. There were zero hobos. Actually, I encountered no one on the trail except a group of teenagers fresh out of high school having picnics with beer and weed, purposefully trying to rid themselves of innocence. I sauntered down a pedestrian bridge that crossed over the highway and made my way to where the waterfall plunged into the river. I took a moment and watched the shade from the sunset creep up over the top of the bluff. Instead of climbing the steps back up to the top, I took the walkway parallel to Highway 99 and the railroad at the bottom.

At the end of the trail, the walkway dipped downward into a pedestrian tunnel. *Well, this is creepy*—I thought as I approached. I couldn't see around the corner. It was dark and I was very alone. I took a deep breath, grabbed the sharpest of my keys, and hoped that armed transients thirsty for God-knows-what weren't lurking around the bend.

They weren't. It was a short empty tunnel, but it was graced by a massive amount of original graffiti and personal inscriptions from evocative to meaningless significance. It was dark, but I could still read. I dragged my hand lightly over the cold concrete, taking note of a few of the quotations. After ten feet I saw light again. I turned the corner inside the strange, hidden tunnel and emerged onto one of the main downtown avenues. My eyes adjusted to light again.

I looked directly to my right and there was Black Beauty waiting for me.

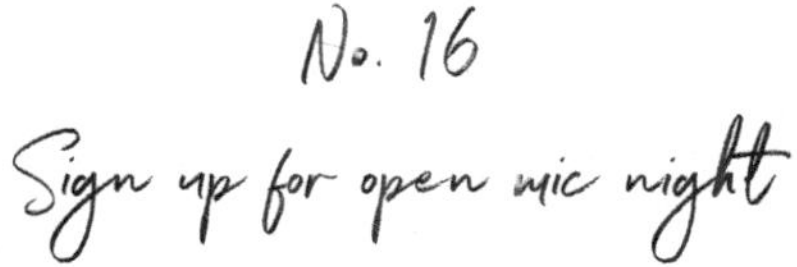

I drove north on Highway 99 toward downtown Portland, somewhat determined to bust out the last Date right then and there, eager to erase the cancelled Hinge-date/green-tea/ mic-less open mic debacle. I was so excited at the prospect of finishing 48 of my 50 that I parked near a theater that I knew had a comedy open mic and walked in just in time to see the start of the show. The sign-up was full, however.

I got a beer and situated myself in the front row. At least I could do research for the last of the difficult Dates. I had banked enough courage after watching ten three-minute sets that I thought to myself—*Yeah, I can totally do this. I can come back next week and try*—when a familiar face appeared onstage. Tinder Fail #2, aka 1998 Justin Timberlake, took the microphone (See Side Story #4).

*Holy shit…*I tucked my head down hoping to God he didn't see me. After the MC identified him as a frequent host of the multi-weeknight comedy event series, I decided I needed to go somewhere else to cross off No. 16.

July 7th, 2015—There are different styles of open mic nights. There's the singing kind and there's the poetry slam kind, which I unfairly make fun of. I know I shouldn't, it takes balls to get up onstage and do anything in front of other people—no matter if it's terrible lines of iambic pentameter illustrating some guy's tear-stained struggle to get over his ex-boyfriend and move on with the ultimate dream of becoming the best hacky-sack performer of all time. (I'm such a bitch sometimes. God, why don't I just go write a damn book about my own struggles and leave everyone else alone?)

In preparation to take the stage and a stab at the funny, I watched an unhealthy amount of Amy Schumer videos on YouTube. Then I watched all the episodes of her Comedy Central sketch comedy show *Inside Amy Schumer*. Then I watched any videos available of Amy Schumer speaking. Then I developed the biggest woman crush ever and posted her *Trainwreck* trailer to my Facebook page with delirious anticipation.

With my Tinder Distractions as pure inspiration, along with a phenomenally sad website I found called Tinderseduction.com, I developed a four-minute set that spewed self-deprecating anecdotal evidence of my romantic failures. I rehearsed for a few days, and the anxiety built to a point of uncontrollability. I had to buy new antiperspirant.

I found an open mic at a tiny dive bar where I was *certain* I would find *no one* I ever knew, or met, or tried to sleep with in my life. They had a Tuesday night open mic, and this night I was hopeful that the gigantic Portland's Funniest Person Competition Finals would horde all the important and talented local comedians, including 1998 Justin Timberlake from Tinder Distraction #2. I put on a skirt to feel hot and drove over to the hole in the wall bar. I parked Black Beauty and recited my lines a few more times, using the timer on my phone. I didn't want the imaginary (or real) gigantic hook to come out of the wings and pull me offstage. I felt solid enough to exit my car and walk to the entrance. I approached the dingy tavern seeing two elderly dudes smoking at a table outside and a young woman taking out the umbrellas from the other tables as it got dark. The young woman turned around and saw me.

"Oh hey! Marie!"

What the crap.

"Hey, Rachel," I said, in pure astonishment. Rachel (celebrity casting Rachel Leigh Cook) was a bartender at the Corner Bar, as well as at this one apparently.

Shit. More evidence I have not an alcohol problem but a bar problem. I can't go to a new fucking bar without seeing anyone I know, let alone someone else who has poured me a drink before. I followed her inside the dive.

"The usual?" she asked me.

"Um, well, I was actually here for the open mic," I admitted hesitantly.

"Oh! It's cancelled, sorry," she said, "There's a big contest or something tonight."

"Yeah, I know," I said hiding my crumpled-up paper. "Okay, the usual then."

I talked with Rachel a bit. The local drunkard sitting at the bar talked to me for a while and touched my arm too much for my taste. I was about to down my drink and take off for home, my spirits dashed, when three young guys slapped their palms on the bar and announced to the six other people inside the place:

"Your attention, please! We are going to do a mic-less open mic here in five minutes. We know the official one was cancelled, but we want to make you laugh anyway. See you in a bit!"

Rachel flashed me a look that said — *OMG you have to do it.*

The local drunkard who looked like the Portland-version of Jack Sparrow agreed.

I ordered another drink and decided to go for it.

Comedian Dudes #1 and #2 were buddies who recently moved to Portland to try to get their feet in the comedy door. Dude #3 had a similar story. All of them commiserated that they weren't celebrity cool enough to get invited to the big contest that night. Then they all encouraged me to step up to the makeshift stage in front of an imaginary mic and yell my mediocre jokes at them — which I did in Tim Gunn "make it work" fashion.

I was petrified. I was sweating. I was elated that I got a few laughs. I was relieved when the four minutes were over and happy when they all clapped and patted me on the back. I was surprised when the three Dudes bought me a drink after and the four of us took selfies together and posted on Facebook after friending each other, marking the Infamous Mic-less Open Mic Night for comedic posterity.

The Dudes asked me to come back the following week to try it for real. I told them Mic-less Open Mic would count for my List, and I was wary to return and spill my guts for vulnerable jesting glory again. Though, I did think about it.

After forty-nine Dates with myself, I realized I had morphed into the kind of woman I knew I already was deep down—poised, brazenly shameless, and intrepid. Hell yeah! Who needs a microphone when the only person's opinion you really take stock in is your own?

Maybe I'll go back and open mic again sometime. Maybe not. All I know is I sacked up and did it—the last of the Dates that required bravery and strain.

Forty-nine done!

I looked at my List with wonder, pride, and some small amount of sorrow the journey was now coming to a close—but completely elated I had made it this far, and thrilled beyond belief I would hang the finished List on my bedroom wall in the near future.

I had one celebratory Date left.

Side Story #9
The Dufus Reappearance

June 28, 2015—Summer has returned. It's effing hot. I'm surpassing a lifetime record of going days without wearing long jeans. I guess the Pacific Northwest is getting the better end out of global warming; plenty of ninety-plus days and we still have drinking water without drought restrictions. Maybe we'll grow oranges here in another ten years.

It was the end of a five day off-work stretch, during which

I had: played flag football, sung karaoke at the Corner Bar, taken a second solo road trip to Hood River where I hiked five miles alone, visited two new breweries, rafted the White Salmon River including the navigation of a Class V waterfall with six perfect strangers, *and* I rode my bike seven miles with 9,000 other crazy persons in Portland's World Naked Bike Ride wearing nothing but socks, shoes, and a mermaid wig.[57] It was a terrifying yet liberating experience.

On this lazy Sunday afternoon, a day after returning home from Hood River, I left my hot apartment for another Portland Timbers home match. Usually, for a big game like this one, I'd arrive at the stadium way before kickoff to snag a wristband guaranteeing me early entrance into the stadium. Today, after a week of fun in the sun, I was exhausted and thought sitting up in the rafters in the shade instead of the mosh pit in direct sunlight might be a nice change—which also meant I had the whole day to recover at home, do laundry, and get ready for the work week. Ah, adulthood. With only twenty minutes until kickoff, I rushed out of the house and down the street to the train stop, texting my brothers that I was on my way.

The train made one stop before I felt a tap on my shoulder.

"Wow, you're as late to the game as I am!" Dufus exclaimed.

"Hey!" I replied, surprised but not floored. He was always late to games, to everything really.

It was the first time I had seen him since he gave me the Empty Fucking Picture Frame. Miraculously, ten months had gone by without us running into each other, despite still

---

57   If you live in Portland, or anywhere that does this, you should do it— at least once in your life. https://pdxwnbr.org/

living eight blocks apart and keeping somewhat overlapping social circles. I was thankful for the lengthy absence, for obvious reasons, and because my initial reaction upon seeing the dumbass that broke my heart was not hatred or anger, it was mostly bewilderment and curiosity and… joy.

Wait, what? Hang on, I'm hugging the guy.

What the fuck am I doing? Punch him! Punch him!!!

I have to say, only 5% of me wanted to punch him. Yeah, we awkwardly hugged. We spent the rest of the train ride exchanging essentials on our lives. I recounted the above recent solo trip to Hood River and Naked Bike Ride adventure, to which he was astounded and congratulated me. He told me details about his life which made me profoundly thank God/whatever Deity would listen that I was *not* with him anymore. Twenty minutes later we walked inside the stadium, hugged again saying to each other, "Don't be a stranger!" and waved goodbye as the Timbers Army chants swelled. I met my brothers in the upper 200s sections in the shade just before kickoff.

Genuinely, I held almost no malice towards him. Almost. I don't think I'll ever get rid of that 5%, but seeing him didn't bother me. I was honestly glad he was doing fine. I was even gladder I was doing fabulously well and got to tell him about how awesome my life was without him. I was still riding the high from the Naked Bike Ride the night before. I was so close to being done with the List. I was the most tan I had been since high school and just happened to put on a skirt for the game and felt amazing, and maybe some part of Dufus felt regret. Also, I had a remarkably great first date with an amazing new guy just the day beforehand. I was over Dufus. I had moved on a long time ago and was just now fully realizing it. Whatever the case, I made it through the awkward post-breakup run-in with flying colors and went on with my life.

Dufus, on the other hand, texted me a few weeks later asking to meet up over drinks.

Sigh.

After years of knowing one another, and being together, it was difficult to 1.) Resist the urge to swig a sweet taste of old friendship and 2.) Miss any opportunity to show the person what a fuck-up he was to let me go in the first place.

Yep, that 5% is pretty permanent.

Just a week after I finished the mic-less open-mic in No. 16, I met Dufus for beers somewhere in the Pearl District and the two above needs were indeed satiated. His often stupid comments and rather alarming revelations about his midlife crisis further reinforced to me I was entirely better off on my own. Conversely, talking over a few pints of beer was like putting on a pair of old, treasured sneakers—frayed and worn but that still fit well. The result was a kind of bittersweet sadness. I knew I was putting on and taking off those shoes for the last time ever and chucking them in the trash.

Not everyone gets closure with previous relationships. I guess I had to feel lucky. Of course, we took the train back to our end of downtown (*Ugh…maybe I should move*) while I halfway listened to his idiotic banter and contemplated the Universe's strange manner of making Dufus magically reappear with one Date left to go at the end of my List journey. How serendipitous is that, right? Was it a reward? Or was it a challenge?

It was a goodbye.

It was the last shovel of dirt on the coffin that was saved

for just the right moment. I know Dufus didn't see it that way, but I did.

I walked home mentally barefoot, ready to end this journey and start a new one.

No. 50

Put on a dress. Take out some friends. Buy them drinks. Have a great night. Then frame this epic List, because congratulations, you are a certified badass.

July 30th, 2015—Night of a Blue Moon.

For the illustrious finale, I chose a swanky bar at the top of the Nines Hotel called *Departure*. Honestly, I chose it for its upscale classiness—but the day of, I realized just how amusingly the name and my occasion corresponded—an ironic fortune I whole-heartedly appreciated. Thank you, Universe. Six of my best gal pals who invested in the List joined me for the high-spirited ending, accompanied by four bottles of champagne I put on my tab. Truly, those women exceed my admiration in every possible way and to them I cannot overstate my gratitude.

I'm unable to justly express how full of happiness I felt—for so many reasons, besides the delicious champagne. For one, finishing something I set out to do—for achieving the stated objective of Rebooting myself inside out.

For not letting the rock bottoms falter me. For undertaking everything between lows and highs. For not defining myself or my contentment based on anyone else.

For gaining closure with Dufus. For chronicling the

journey and writing the longest document my laptop has ever saved. For being brave enough to share it with friends and family, and eventually all of you.

For refusing to settle for mediocrity.

For unreservedly accepting my own special flavor of nerdy quirkiness and fallible wit.

For being unapologetic.

For getting my hands dirty.

For facing fear straight on.

For never giving up on myself.

And for having—absolutely—the time of my life.

Epilogue

August 14th, 2015—I stood on a great lawn with thousands of other concert-goers watching Dave Grohl bust out *The Best of You* on his guitar with a broken leg. The travelling music festival "Gentlemen of the Road Stopover Tour" shacked up in Walla Walla, Washington for the weekend boasting several top-notch musical acts like the Foo Fighters, the Flaming Lips, the Vaccines, the Tune-Yards, and many more.

I went with my friend Jennifer (celebrity casting: Jennifer Lawrence) who was one of the singular ladies drinking champagne with me at No. 50. We camped with about eight thousand other music festival enthusiasts on a golf course, drank beer, slept in a tent, and suffered long Porta-Potty lines and no-campfire stipulations so we could experience the absolute brilliance of the festival host band the following night, international phenoms Mumford & Sons. During my very favorite song of theirs I cried, earnestly clutched my chest, and beat my fist in the air in euphoric groupie fashion.

It was my Woodstock, and I was so ecstatic to be

experiencing something of such mega proportions on the exact one-year anniversary of embarking on the List journey. It was so fitting, watching Dave Grohl play for hours onstage resting his casted leg on a stool, his message so clear: even if you trip on your own feet and utterly shatter your ankle, you get out there and jam like a rock star anyway. The show must go on. The metaphor pleased me, and I congratulated myself for also trekking onward in spite of pain, infirmity, and woe—though I can't exactly compare my ordeal to Dave Grohl's broken ankle. Pain, in its many forms, is all subjective anyhow.

Here are the stats: It took me 350 days to cross off all 50 Dates. While it spread over twelve months of the calendar, most of the Dates were completed in September 2014 (13), followed by November (9), October (7), December and August (4 each), three in February 2015, two each in March/May/June/July, and one in both January and April.

More than a handful of the Dates were repeated. I fully accomplished No. 12 by doing the Naked Bike Ride. I got a spa membership after No. 13. I secured tickets to see St. Lucia in concert again (No. 24). I went river kayaking and rafting additional times (No. 5) and my enthusiasm for Powell's Books (No. 43) and Buffalo Exchange (No. 44) never abated—much to the dismay of my credit card. I cooked the meal from the cooking class several more times for myself and others (No. 11). I absolutely love my new car which is already dirty from outdoor adventures. I stopped counting the number of solo road trips (No. 46)—and I think tackling the idea of saving for a property purchase is not entirely out of reach (No. 45). Many of the other Dates I elected not to reprise. They seem like they happened just the way they were supposed to (i.e., No. 3 and No. 16).

I am ultimately learning that the 50 Dates reaped rewards much greater than I originally thought possible. I'm not sure what I expected at the beginning of all this. I think, initially, a lot of it had to do with purely needing a distraction from the emotional hurt, but I wound up winning so much more than just getting over a break-up.

There is no better way to put it than this: I am so in love with my life.

The last time I cried, other than from the heartfelt musical orgasm provided by Mumford & Sons, was when I watched Jon Stewart say goodbye to *The Daily Show* this month. My social calendar is currently jam-packed with happy hours, work-related projects, family get-togethers, and outdoor activities galore. Coming up, the rest of the summer plans include a rafting trip down the Deschutes River, road trips to the coast and to Central Oregon, more Timbers games, more *Star Wars* theme parties, and Wednesday night karaoke at the Corner Bar has become quite a habit.

This fall I plan to attend my ten-year high school reunion and then hop a plane a few weeks later to a Third World country with a team of other medical professionals/ perfect strangers to provide general medicine clinics for the underserved rural population. I figure, I just spent a whole year reworking myself; it's time to get my hands dirty by really making a difference for someone else in a place where needs revolve around basic human necessity and people don't have the luxury of dating themselves. I've been dreaming about going on a medical mission trip like this since junior high school. I never would have had the guts to do something this big—particularly by myself—in my lifetime pre-Reboot.

Typhoid vaccine and malaria prophylaxis here I come!

I can say I completed 36 of the Dates purely on my own without friends or others helping me accomplish the feat. Pretty good I think, hilarious that I originally thought I'd do all 50 without help. I would be utterly remiss if I didn't write a heartfelt thank you to those who helped me complete the other 14, and for being so supportive during the Reboot process. My endless gratitude and love go out to the celebrities of my life:

- Rashida Jones and her husband Seth Rogan in Bend, Oregon
- Rashida's dad Michael Keaton
- my amazing friend Blake Lively and her boyfriend Jake Johnson
- my good buddy Adam Brody for encouraging me to "stay on the horse"
- my Geek Trivia partner Jewel Staite
- my two best college girlfriends Julia Stiles and Maya Rudolph who suffered all the boy drama via email and Skype
- my friend/wine connoisseur/solo traveler extraordinaire/ F-word Queen Emma Stone
- my esteemed friend/colleague/Instagram-addict Cate Blanchett
- my dear also-single aunt Melissa McCarthy
- the wacky neighborhood karaoke crew at The Corner Bar, celebrity casting: The Muppets' Dr. Teeth and the Electric Mayhem
- the Timbers Army/107ist for being the awe-inspiring organization that it is

- Underdog Sports for taking lots of my money over the years and creating a corn hole league
- my beloved brothers Andy Samberg and Topher Grace, my sister-in-law Natalie Portman, and my sister Aubrey Plaza and soon-to-be brother-in-law Russell Brand
- my mother Sally Field for being eternally supportive of me, for reading drafts of my book and probably sections I explicitly told her to skip
- my dad Bill Murray for being a light in my life, and (hopefully) forgiving me for unambiguously detailing my 20-something debauchery in the form of widely-available prose
- my friend Susan Sarandon for being one of the coolest ladies I know and for inspiring me to take charge of my own journey to happiness
- And lastly, my six extraordinary friends who attended No. 50 and endured my four-bottles-of-champagne speeches, hugs, and kisses: Cate Blanchett, Kristin Wiig, Blake Lively, Ellie Kemper, Jennifer Lawrence, and Amanda Seyfried. It would have been impossible to complete all 50 without you.

Once again, I have NOT actually met ANY of the celebrities used as placeholders in this book, and the actions of said characters do not necessarily reflect my opinion of the real-life people, especially those robust male actors I used to illustrate all the gentlemen I dated from deplorable to lukewarm. It was absolutely nothing personal Jason Segel, Josh Charles, Joel McHale, Jai Courtney, Ashton Kutcher, John Krasinski, Jake Gyllenhaal, and 1998 Justin Timberlake.

For the record, none of those guys have reemerged. I did receive an astonishing apology text from Jake Gyllenhaal eight months after the fact, but that's it. And as far as my "guy-atus" goes…(*laughs*)…well, the rumors are true. I have legitimately started exclusively dating someone besides myself. Julia's Rom-Com Theory proved only slightly true in this instance; but yes, a grown-up man has indeed come along and while his surprising and most welcome arrival in my life is an added bonus to an already blissful wrap-up of this journey, it is all the feelings of exhilaration—everything I described in No. 50—that really made this the most worthwhile adventure in my life to date. Even if it doesn't ultimately work out with this new guy, I'll always have this one-year slice of my life hitting the reset button to feel proud of.[58]

In actuality, I shouldn't ever stop Dating myself, no matter how my life turns out. The only person I'll ever truly need to live with forever after is me, and I think I'm pretty badass now. Not that I was seriously uncool before, I just I feel like now I should carry a club member card or something (See Appendix C).

My emotional gas tank is no longer void like it was a year ago, and while I'll keep the scars I've sustained I definitely feel whole again, in control of where I'm going and how I feel. And in the supremely highly unlikely case I somehow forget what exactly this feels like, I can just look up at my bedroom wall where The Epic List hangs in a simple white wooden frame—right next to where I put a photo of me and my six girlfriends all dressed up at Departure/Date No. 50—square in the same 5x7 now-not-so-Empty Fucking Picture Frame.

---

58   It's so true. I do still feel very proud of this year, and I carry all those penultimate feelings with me even today, years later. Oh, also, I totally married that guy. ☺

My life is the opposite of empty, and it is more than conceivable I have the capability to keep it that way. Echoing Susan Sarandon, my friend I mentioned way back in the Prologue, I wish this kind of feeling for all my friends and loved ones, and for all of you out there who were curious enough to pick up and read my little escapade, whatever your reasons for initial interest may have been.

I can say I'm excited to see what comes next. I'm not sure I'll feel the need to write another autobiographical memoir—but stranger things have happened.

To paraphrase one of my favorite Klingon warriors: where the tides of fortune take us, no one can know.

Here's to good sailing.

Appendix A: Things You May Also Like

Books

- Brown, Kelly Williams. 2013. *Adulting: how to become a grown-up in 468 easy(ish) steps.*
- Ansari, Aziz, and Eric Klinenberg. 2015. *Modern romance.*
- Behrendt, Greg, and Amiira Ruotola-Behrendt. 2009. *It's called a break-up because it's broken: the smart girl's breakup buddy.* London: HarperElement. https://overdrive.com/search?q=0019F304-86FE-4860-B432-8EE6D3A6DFEE.
- Strayed, Cheryl. 2012. *Wild: from lost to found on the Pacific Crest Trail.* New York: Alfred A. Knopf. *Part 3 introductory quote used with permission from the author.*

Articles

- Buzzfeed List: *Life in Your Early Twenties vs Your Late Twenties*
- http://buzzfeed.com/jessicamisener/life-in-your-early-twenties-vs-your-late-twenties#.bsK6MvyaW
- *21 Struggles That Are Way Too Real For Every Girl Who's Online Dated*
- http://buzzfeed.com/remeepatel/its-just-full-on-penis#.db6A97LZ8

Films

- *The Break-up*
- *500 Days of Summer*
- *The Goonies*—have you really not seen this? *Goonies never say die!* Go watch it right now.
- Television
- *New Girl*, Season 4, Episode 2, "Dice"

- *Broad City*
- *Inside Amy Schumer*
- *Geeks Who Drink,* hosted by Zachary Levi (now defunct)

<u>Mobile Apps</u>

- Tinder…if you're single and looking for questionably-healthy fun
- Instagram…then follow the account *Tindernightmares*
- Airbnb…then for God's sake book a trip somewhere

Appendix B: Drunken Star Wars Cocktails

For the absolute Nerds out there who like the idea of mixing alcohol and science fiction, behold: recipes to wet the lips from a galaxy far far away. By August, we had *subthemes* for the theme parties. May the Force be with you and your hangover.

The Anakin Chaiwalker (Episode I, February)

- Hot water (or milk)
- Chai tea concentrate
- Butterscotch liqueur
- Brandy
- Star anise

*Over the stove, bring milk/water and chai tea concentrate to a simmer. Fill a mug halfway and add equal parts butterscotch liqueur and brandy. Garnish with star anise.

The Palpatino Cherry (Episode II, April)

- Freshly squeezed lime juice from ½ lime
- Black cherry cola
- Maraschino cherries +juice
- Bourbon
- Ground nutmeg

*Squeeze lime juice over ice. Add black cherry cola and desirable amount of bourbon. Stir. Top with a little juice from the maraschino cherry jar. Add a cherry and a sprinkle of nutmeg to garnish.

Darth Vaderade (Episode III, June) *altered from existing cocktail found on the internet*

- Grape Gatorade
- Sierra Mist, or similar lemon-lime pop

- Coconut rum

*Mix contents as desired, college party punch style. Really, this recipe should be read as Gatorade + alcohol.

Mai-TIE Fighters (Episode IV Luau "Lei the Force Be with You," August)

- Orange juice
- Pineapple juice
- Coconut rum (i.e. Malibu)
- Dark rum (i.e. Trader Vic's Mai Tai blend)
- Pineapple chunks and maraschino cherries

*Mix orange juice and pineapple juice equally in tea cooler for easy serving. Add one shot each (or preferable amount of alcohol) of coconut rum and dark rum. Stir lightly. Add fruity TIE fighter garnish (cut hexagonal pieces of pineapple, make a sandwich with a cherry middle, and secure with toothpick).

Dago-Blood Bath (Episode V Zombie Apocalypse, October)

- White wine
- Blood orange juice mixer
- Champagne

*Mix contents in punch bowl with ice and cinnamon sticks. Add simple syrup if too tart.

The Jolly Ewok of Shame (Episode VI Ugly Sweater Jedi, December)

- Hot chocolate
- Kahlua
- Peppermint schnapps

*Mix desired levels of each liqueur and schnapps in mug of hot chocolate

Appendix C: A Blank List

1. ______________________________
2. ______________________________
3. ______________________________
4. ______________________________
5. ______________________________
6. ______________________________
7. ______________________________
8. ______________________________
9. ______________________________
10. ______________________________
11. ______________________________
12. ______________________________
13. ______________________________
14. ______________________________
15. ______________________________
16. ______________________________
17. ______________________________
18. ______________________________
19. ______________________________
20. ______________________________
21. ______________________________
22. ______________________________
23. ______________________________
24. ______________________________
25. ______________________________
26. ______________________________
27. ______________________________
28. ______________________________

29. ____
30. ____
31. ____
32. ____
33. ____
34. ____
35. ____
36. ____
37. ____
38. ____
39. ____
40. ____
41. ____
42. ____
43. ____
44. ____
45. ____
46. ____
47. ____
48. ____
49. ____
50. ____

BADASS

This card carrier is an official badass, as evidenced by a personal feat that can be described in 50 different ways.

Special Acknowledgements

My heartfelt thanks go to Kelly Lynne Schaub for her editing expertise, Kim Cooper Findling for her encouragement, Dancing Moon Press for guiding me through the publishing process, Face Out Studio's Lindy Martin for the book cover design, and Vanessa Mortinson for photographing my headshot.

Thank you to my family and friends for your steadfast support through the Reboot experience itself and the journey of this book becoming a reality.

Finally, endless love and gratitude go to my husband Rob. I am eternally thankful that you still wanted to date me after I kissed you in my driveway and then abruptly left without explanation to ride a bike with thousands of naked bike riders—*still* loved me after I made you read an early form of this manuscript just months into our courtship—and *still* married me with all my imperfections. Among all my life's stories, our love is the greatest working title. You are a tremendous partner, beyond my wildest hopes and dreams. No more Chautauqua, ever.

Marie MacMillan is a first-time author, podcast host, and registered nurse. When she's not writing prose or working on non-fiction projects, she hosts a healthcare-themed podcast, *Head-to-Toe*. She lives in Portland, Oregon with her husband and son.

The Reboot: 50 Dates with Myself won 2nd Place in the Memoir Category at the 2017 Pacific Northwest Writers Association Literary Contest. Marie also writes short stories and articles about nursing and healthcare. Learn more at mariemacmillan.com

Made in the USA
Monee, IL
14 January 2022